THE LAST OF SEVEN
PART II

The Last of Seven
Part II

Completed Works and Sketches
from My Life in Art

by a former President of the Royal Watercolour Society

ERNEST GREENWOOD
ARCA PPRWS

BRUSHINGS FARM HOUSE PUBLICATIONS
Ashford

Copyright © Ernest Greenwood 2007

First published 2007

Published by the author, Mr Ernest Greenwood
35 Lakeside Place, Chapel Road, Hothfield
Ashford, Kent TN25 4LN.

All rights reserved.
No part of this publication may be reproduced or transmitted in any form or by any means, electronic or mechanical, including photocopy, recording or any information storage and retrieval system, without permission in writing from the publisher.

Book design and production for the publisher by
Bookprint Creative Services, <www.bookprint.co.uk>
Printed in Great Britain.

To My Wife

CONTENTS

	Acknowledgements	9
	Preface	11
	Introduction	13
I	The Sketches	17
II	Watercolour Painting	45
III	Oil Painting	97
IV	The Drawings	121
V	Additional Works	149
	Conclusion	169
	Postscript	187

ACKNOWLEDGEMENTS

I have great pleasure in acknowledging the value of my many American friends who have enriched my life immeasurably. To Dan Leach, collector and connoisseur, in whose company I have spent many happy hours. To Dr. Kim Hiashi who, in his piano recitals has given great pleasure to so many individuals and charitable organisations. To Dr. Walter and Mrs Gillespie, John and Martha Riley, Ray Vasquez, Daniel O'Neill, Dr. June Sprague, Art and Vicky McGregor, Debbie and A.V. Bittecar who with many others have given us warm hospitality and true friendship.

Doreen Goodrick has been an understanding friend from our early Swan Hellenic days. I know no one who can tell an anecdote imbuing it with such penetrating humour; if only these wonderful stories had been recorded. Margaret and Philip Pearce have also added greatly to our cruising experiences.

I particularly wish to thank Hazel Fulford for her helpful and perspicacious reading of my manuscript.

Finally, I must thank Bookprint Creative Services for their valuable, generous help in all matters concerning the publisher's requirements.

PREFACE

Extracts from *Profile of Ernest Greenwood* PPRWS by Maurice Sheppard PPRWS

The sixth of his parents' seven children, Ernest well remembers his walks with his mother along the mill ponds and hop gardens of the River Cray. Also as a child he was quite decided on what he thought of as good. As a five-year-old he murmered 'More! More Frank!' in response to a performance of Beethoven's lovely 'Spring' Violin Sonata played in his parents' parlour by a family friend.

Disposed to poetry as well as philosophy in his teens, Ernest graduated at the very earliest possible age from the Royal College of Art. He was only 21. His professors there were Sir William Rothenstien and Gilbert Spencer. Extending his studies first at the British School at Rome and then back at the Royal College he spent a further year studying etching under Malcolm Osborne.

[. . .]

Visiting Ernest's studio high up in the 'King posts' of the roof of his sixteenth century hall house, it is rows of bound drawing books that most delight me. Here in a fine, often brittle, line of pencil or more often ink the whole world of Ernest's imagination comes to life. His travels, be they those when he was in the services or those undertaken during his Swan-Hellenic 'journeys around the Med' as a scholar-guide and host are all recorded in some way. A canal barge holiday in France can look, over a whole drawing book, as tight-packed and intensive a mental journey as those notebooks we see so much of by nineteenth century artists.

But what happens to all these studies? I have said that Ernest has a strong disposition to philosophy and poetry and indeed his appreciation of those thinkers and poets who have allowed their thoughts to crystallise slowly have given him his own creative method. He allows the many concentrated images he has so carefully drawn to melt and rearrange themselves in his mind's eye.

One of his largest watercolour mixed-media pieces can take up to four years to arrive at a satisfactory balance and conclusion which will take into account not just the topographical starting point but other related images and forms and atmospheres.

[. . .]

If, indeed, Ernest in his painting is 'Elgarian – autumnal' in feel it is to an Englishness of spirit that his work turns our mind.

I hope the publication of *Part I* and *Part II* as separate books in no way prevents the reader from seeing my life and work as constituting one narrative.

INTRODUCTION

When passing into the twenty-first century I became aware of what it had meant for me. Nothing could provide a stronger contrast in the social, moral and political issues that continue to occupy the minds of many people; these changes apply not least to the arts which have passed through so many phases, one after the other in quick succession. All art schools believed the basic, essential thing was to acquire sound draughtsmanship by a concentrated study of the nude figure assisted by a working knowledge of artistic anatomy, both subjects I found particularly absorbing, occupying all my thought and energy. There was, as a result of this traditional training, opposition to the revolutionary work and thinking that was creating a great movement in London and Europe which was emerging from the drawings and paintings by three dominant personalities: Picasso, Braque and Matisse. They completely discarded and rejected all the research done in the Italian Renaissance in unearthing principles of creative design from the many studies of classical sculpture and literature to which scholars and artists had given their time and thought.

The mysticism of Leonardo, the power of Michelangelo culminating in the authority of Raphael had planted an indelible pattern for so many painters to use for 250 years. It was bound to exhaust itself, as it did towards the end of the nineteenth century. It was in this tradition we received our art education and as a very young inexperienced student I had nothing with which to compare it. An art magazine called *Design* was the only link with the new philosophy in London, sparked off by Roger Fry, but the headmaster of Gravesend school completely opposed any such movement and cancelled the contribution to the magazine.

Draughtsmanship remained the main purpose of work in the life-class. Demonstrations by three members of staff were found to be obviously lacking in an understanding or ability to draw form. A senior student from another art school (who had been instructed by a master draughtsman), taught me the fundamental difference between copying thoughtlessly and drawing as a search for a grasp of form and space as a three-dimensional concept. From now onwards my drawings began to show not only skill but some ability to place the figure or other objects in relationship to its environment, the first step towards painting to which our studies in anatomy and perspective contributed. One of the essentials absent from these early years was any kind of historical information from an art historian. This would have stimulated our practical work.

I do not think any of us had any idea of the importance of Europe or Italy as it was in the sixteenth century or why the Duchy of Burgundy played such an important roll in art and commerce. My reading centred on the Italian Renaissance, its political, territorial and religious upheavals while at the same time I was fascinated by the great works in architecture and painting which were only slowly emerging from the formal, decorative idiom of Byzantine to the beginnings of a move towards liberalism and freedom from centuries of Imperial and priesthood dominance.

No major movement of people across Europe had taken place without the spread of their culture. This is clearly seen in the dissemination of the Francs, part of the great immigration from the north into France, Lombardy and Spain. The churches, cathedrals and other monastic building of the eleventh and twelfth centuries, like great footprints, mark the occupation of the countries which grew from the ashes of the Roman Empire into a new beginning for Europe – the Romanesque. This Romanesque was a period of original creations in architecture, sculpture, the decorative arts in jewellery and book illustration which were influenced by the peoples from northern Europe and the remnants of the great achievements of the west. In the following centuries the remarkable change over the whole area into European Gothic resulted from new building techniques coupled with the gradual perfection of painting in an oil medium for major works, rather than in fresco as in Italy.

By the time a certain Florentine citizen, Cimabue, was at work in 1240–1302, the change in painting was becoming apparent – a movement which accelerated as the fourteenth century advanced. Perhaps the most powerful artist to emerge, however, was Giotto (1266–1337), another Florentine. He was found by Cimabue who took him to Florence, brought him up from boyhood and with his own instruction planted the seeds of the Renaissance. which thus had its beginning in an artist who broke the bonds imposed by previous centuries.

I

THE SKETCHES

MANY OF THE DRAWINGS in my sketch books were done for the sheer pleasure of employing different techniques as the subject seemed to demand.

Drawings can provide contrasting possibilities. Two of mine show how the owners of a chateau had long gone past their halcyon days. The large building was lived in all alone by a spinster and her horse. The gates from the garden across the moat were rusted into a crooked mass of iron work. The present occupier must have lived in a mere fraction of available accommodation which was emphasised by a packet of Persil, prominent on a shelf above the sink which must have been the kitchen on the ground floor. The thirteenth century building was complete, never having had to suffer at the hands of soldiers or vandals. Because of neglect there was a sadness hanging over the house and garden, weeds now dominated areas that had once been carefully tended flower beds, the outbuildings were in a sad state of dilapidation There must have been a period when the house and gardens rang with chatter and laughter of happy people and much loved children but those days had gone for ever.

Drawings bear the imprint of personality; they also reveal the purpose for which the drawing is made. This is demonstrated by the difference between an architectural drawing and a study of the nude made by Rembrandt. A portrait drawing by Holbein or Ingres not only records the sitter as a person but includes the individuality, by style, of the artist. My twenty or more books of sketches formed an illustrated diary filled with drawings, ranging from very slight notes to more complete statements. Every drawing had significance for me. In my extensive travels the sketch book was the most convenient way of collecting material for future use. I therefore carried with me a variety of drawing media. The black chalk used for my sketch of Aegina reflected the drama which was how I saw this Greek temple in the fading evening light and made this medium so appropriate. Amongst the mixed collection of drawing materials I always included three bottles of wash grey, sepia and grey-blue. When time was short it was a rapid way to record light, pattern and the relative importance of things in terms of area or counter-change. There are also occasions when the matter of relative size can give a subject monumentality.

The casual reader may not be aware of why certain drawing tools are used at given times, which these notes may elucidate. The line expresses much about the scribe as every personal signature demonstrates. Apart from this obvious fact the line can be used by the artist with great sensitivity, to reflect his immediate needs often of an emotional nature, much as a pianist uses the keyboard to express moods, from the dramatic to the lyrical.

Notes to the Sketches

1. The Carcassone restored by Violé le Duc presents, in its entirety, a whole folio of possible drawings. My sketch suggests a way of using the charcoal, wash and candle wax to provide potential material I never used.

2. The scale and proportions of this view of Granada were very impressive. It was my intention to wash a single tone over the huge wall, but the drawing in pencil remained untouched.

3. This landscape drawing in pen and Indian ink, overlooking the landscape from Olympia demonstrates the use to which I have tried to gain variety from the medium.

4. This rapid note in pencil, done in a matter of a minute or two, was a study for a large painting which included these women busy on the riverside on washing day. (*See also* **No.12**)

5. Mykonos. The intense light on whitewashed walls makes any surface at right angles to the light, windows or open doors, look black. The pattern this can produce is seen in the drawing, a phenomenon I found most interesting.

'Glass of wine' – a little drawing in black silhouette.

6. The donkey, drawn when crossing the ferry at Jerbar. Most horses and donkeys are good, patient models. I have used many.

7. A horse fair at Pont de Veau in 1973.

8. An on location sketch of the distant landscape at Olympia using wash, resist and pen. My two visits to Olympia needed some knowledge and imagination to illuminate and give some meaning to the mass of ruins on the site. The Olympic games, celebrated every four years, was in honour of Olympian Zeus,

the traditional dates of the first games being 776 BC. My sketch shows some of the damage caused by an earthquake, capturing the columns as they fell and broke into cheese-like rolls which could be restored. In addition to the work already done since 1973 (when my sketch was made) more reconstruction may have taken place.

9. Black chalk with charcoal and solid white was used to dramatise the subject. Aegina.

10 & 11. Drawing 11 is a much more positive statement made from the clouds passing overhead, casting shadows, something that never happened in Arizona! In this drawing a dramatic mood was made by contrastingly treated surfaces producing a counter-change of dark against light. The draughtsman is geared to catch any atmospheric changes which will make a new work possible.

12. This pencil study of tonal changes in mixed trees on each side of the canal was used in conjunction with the pencil sketch of women washing in the canal, **No. 4**.

13. A still life drawing of a miscellany of shapes made as an end in itself providing considerable pleasure in its execution and so different from **14**. Digby, 'The Crossword'.

14. This was an attempt to record the maximum information at speed. **Digby, 'The Crossword'**.

15. A night in Paros. It was here we saw the sun go down leaving the sky a deep rich indigo. Visitors were few, the regular clientele were all well-known to each other dominating conversation.

16. This portrait was made in ballpoint pen. The line is continuous and unbroken but informative for the draughtsman.

17. Roussillon is a delightful small town built in red sandstone, making this colour-wash appropriate. The variety of tones was obtained by several applications of the one wash, pen being used for textures on walls and shrubs. This drawing was intended to form the basis of a painting but was never used.

18. The most formidable fortified church I have ever seen is the red brick church-cum-fortress in Albi. The city contains some interesting streets one of which provided me with the dramatic silhouette composite picture, featuring the church, now in the family collection. Apart from the church the city is well known for the Toulouse Lautrec museum containing a splendid collection of his work.

19. My portrait drawing of Grace must speak for itself. That I enjoyed the work, just the recording of facts, like the handbag, is quite obvious, so too is the character of the sitter, which one can almost read.

20. Thermesos, 1978 – wash, water and wax.

21. The essential difference in the use of figures in a landscape or a landscape with figures is again, one of scale. Giorgione's Fête Champêtre in the Louvre is a perfect example of classical lyricism and poetic symbolism. The majestic figure on the left pouring water, or some other libation, into the well is an impressive, statue-like creation reminiscent of a Greek Goddess of the mid 4 BC. The back view of the seated woman is all the more mysterious for this reason: is she smiling or in a reverie in response to the strains of the music as one might almost hear in such a landscape?

22. A painting by Watteau may have a similar title but has a different message. The pictures are highly artificial. They reflect the times of frivolity, the luxury and indolence of one part of the nation. There is little ideology: it is playtime, with lovemaking, pretty gestures and rich garments. These ingredients resulted in beautiful little paintings but none better than the work Watteau, produced. Nos. 21 and 22 do, however, illustrate by contrast the times in which Giorgione and Watteau lived.

23. A landscape with figures – **'Picnic on the Dordogne', 1975.**

When travelling to London by train there was always someone to draw, especially as so many went to sleep. The elderly lady I drew one morning had a wonderful face that encapsulated a great wealth of experience with a lovely temperament. She saw I was drawing her which resulted in a most beautifully angelic smile.

'She smiled at me'

24. Santiago was an absorbing short stay. The architecture, covering many centuries, took up all our time and great interest. The hotel we stayed in had been built originally as a palace overlooking the square of remarkably fine example of buildings from the thirteenth century cathedral portal, to the eighteenth century wing of a Rococo building, which I decided to draw. The subject demanded the need to emphasis the rich ornamentation on a strong vertical axis which I think this drawing probably does.

1: *The Carcassone*

2: Granada

3: Olympia

5: *Mykonos*

8: *Olympia*

9: *Aegina*

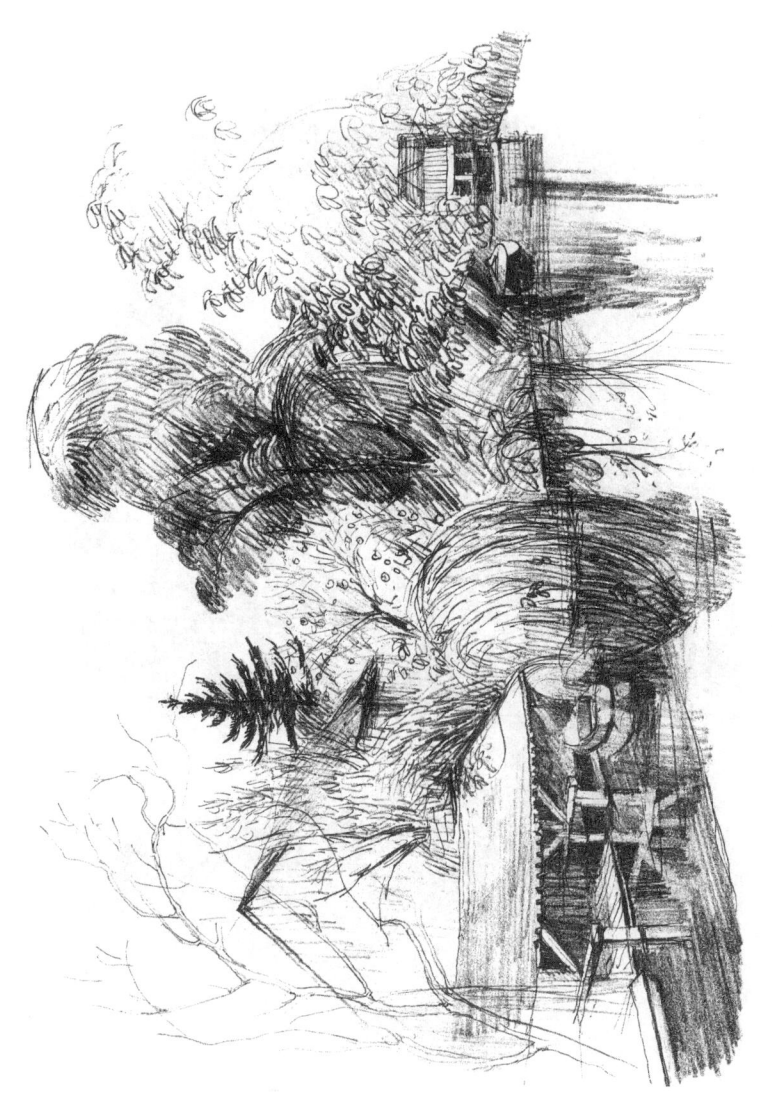

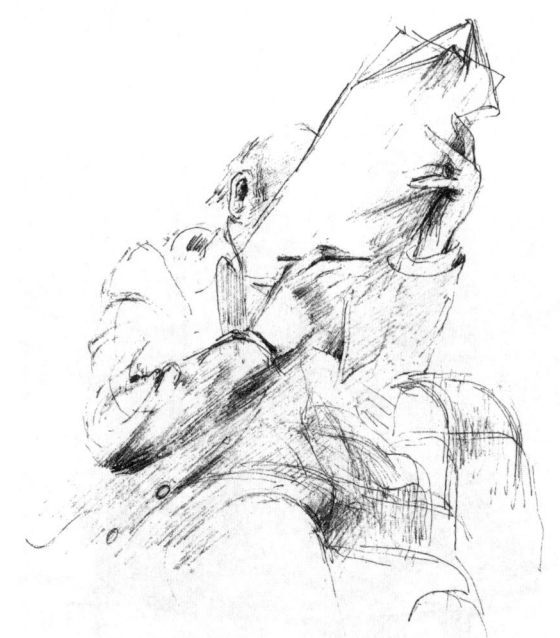

14: Digby, 'The Crossword'

15: Paros

17: *Roussillon*

18: *Albi*

19: *Grace*

20: *Thermesos*

21: Figures in a landscape (Giorgione)

22: A landscape with figures (Watteau)

*23: A landscape with figures – **'Picnic on the Dordogne'**, 1975*

24: *Santiago*

❦ II ❦

WATERCOLOUR PAINTING

When the Royal Watercolour Society (RWS) held its first exhibitions in 1804 a new chapter in English painting was inaugurated. These first exhibitions generated great interest and support through sales, and were thought to be a challenge to oil painting; but in fact watercolour was not essentially an English invention. The great Fresco painting cycles in Italy were executed in watercolour but it was Claude Lorrain (1682), Albrecht Dürer (1528) as well as Van Dyke (1641) who used the medium at about the same time. However, the ancient Egyptians used water colour in papyruses, Chinese painting on silk, illuminated manuscripts in the middle ages, as well as in Elizabethan portraits. The largest and most ambitious use of this medium, and a miracle of preservation, are the complete set of full size designs for tapestries by Raphael (1520) now in the Victoria & Albert museum. These huge works must have required a host of assistants to do all the 'donkey work': prepare the paper, grind all the colours in pestle and mortar, add the right amount of gum, in readiness for the artists use.

As with oil painting, I had no instruction in the use of watercolour. It was not considered a medium to spend any time on, even in the British School in Rome. It was therefore a great surprise when to receive an invitation to apply for membership to the RWS, and an even greater one when I was elected, especially when my work was mainly monochromatic at the time. Although a member of the society, and its President for eight years, I cannot say that I was entirely in agreement with the often-voiced assertion of the greatness of the society. It is the same with the Royal Academy and many other institutions which are supported by loyal members.

For some unexplained reason the use of white was frowned upon by some senior practitioners who assumed that work was only done on white paper. But tinted paper was also used, especially in the fifteenth and sixteenth centuries by Italian draughtsmen, thereby making the use of white necessary. This fact was overlooked when the 'no white paint' doctrine became obsolete. By the time of my retirement the prohibition of the 'white theory' had been repudiated although I had heard the idea of the 'no white theory' approvingly expressed by some. Apart from the above, importance is rightly given to the question of paper: a poor quality paper containing a high proportion of acid, as well as strong sunlight, can be detrimental to watercolours, causing fading, which has happened to some of Turner's watercolours. With oil painting the texture of the canvas from a fine surface to a very coarse grain provides an artist with a wide choice. The same applies to watercolour papers although one particular product is in general use. Because my practice was to work from drawings over a long period I required a rigid surface which could be worked on without any difficulty arising from cockling or tearing, so I found a board of high quality, acid free, that suited my need very well. It enabled me to work on a large scale which I found most satisfying. The six or seven pictures of the 'Canal du Midi' series could not have been produced on location. The three triptychs, of which one is reproduced in *The Watercolour Expert*, is symptomatic of the scale I worked on. The largest, being six foot by four foot – the 'Resurrection' – is reproduced in *Part I*. The original, now rolled up in a Kodak box at Bonhams, has a doubtful future.

The six 'Canal du Midi' pictures were designed from drawings. The three illustrations reproduced show a method of working from a sketch to the final picture. As most of my working hours were spent in the studio I had all the time needed to cogitate, to allow the mind to concentrate on the subject matter, with its many interpretative possibilities. I found working on a series on one theme assisted me to gather the most that was obtainable from the total of the remembered experiences. Experiences fill the mind with images, but not all images can be used for pictorial purposes. The four illustrated here represent the results of my method of working. (Titles and numbers on photographs). In the French series I used a working method as for the French canals, except that more journeys into rural France, covering over twenty-five years, resulted in more drawings and paintings; the former constituting a large proportion of the contents of the sketch books from which many paintings were made.

As mentioned in *Part I*, two of the most fascinating villages we have ever stayed in were Collange la Rouge and Carranac. In each, the visit was long enough to settle down to work. Each one was rich with medieval architecture – ecclesiastical and domestic. Collange la Rouge has a particularly fine Romanesque church. On my first visit a tape was playing church music which gave an indescribable, mystical atmosphere, strongly felt when alone. The ticking clock, the chiming bell caused an involuntary look up into the open base of the tower, where the complicated and extremely skilful carpentry made one wonder how the work was done. Because of the already completed part of the building outside, scaffolding was impossible, as with the spire on Salisbury cathedral, where the carpentry is even more complex, and the geometry perfect. With not one break in the symmetry such a high spire was a marvellous achievement. Collange was wonderful even when we had our second visit but this was in the forties and fifties, before touring bus companies made it a 'must' in their brochures. The little town with its occasional horse-drawn, agricultural traffic must have been a lovely place in which to live. By the church, undercover, were the communal baking ovens and the itinerant whisky still – very primitive equipment which supplied the surrounding families with all the spirits they needed! Carranac was an equally beautiful place, basically built by the river. The little village stimulated the imagination. The motivation to work, to think and to dream, activated by being alone during these working times, when the sensibilities were free to absorb and help in the creation of future pictures, were invaluable. The photographs reproducing some of these paintings are representative of the work done.

These were lovely times especially at dusk, when evening slipped into a night of stars and warmth. The atmosphere was clean and cool, the air fresh and sweet with the perfume of flowering plants. Voices were hushed and movement unhurried by the local occupants dining at tables in the open air, or under sunshades. Wine has a distinguished aroma all its own, especially in Greece where Bacchus was worshipped, although most drinkers are unconscious of the debt owed to this God of Olympus. The smell of wine in the air, the faint drift of smoke from a Gauloises cigarette, combine to induce a complete lassitude, a sense of absolute freedom and peace. It was on such a night that the song of the nightingale confirmed our need to convert hopes into reality. As I emerged from my reverie

I realised that concepts of reality are various and often contradictory. The philosophic doctrine that 'in external perception of the objects immediately known are real', covers many things concerning human existence and experience. Hitler thought power was real. The facts of life are thought real by many – although scientists are proving otherwise. But if reality is related to time then another factor must be taken into consideration. The concept of reality is ephemeral, it has no positive definition because time makes and destroys reality. Time is infinite, the sun shining on us today warmed the dinosaurs; bythis reality, time is now being extended, to an ever greater degree, by space travel.

There is, moreover, the complex combination and arrangement of sounds which make music die at the moment of creation only to be born again through the ears to the mind and sensibilities. The work of the composer, performer and listener all share the experience in different ways. The same should be true with painting: there is the artist, his work and the eyes that look upon the work. As a painting uses visual material as a means of communication – landscape, still life and portraiture – the means take precedence over everything else, with verisimilitude often being the main objective. Great painting can sometimes lose the object(s) in the production of a work of art. Turner's work is a splendid example of this as it changes from illustration in the early drawings and paintings to the last works in which the title and subject pale into insignificance as the use of colour, space and atmosphere move into an imaginative, mysterious world of their own creating. The quality of a society is finally judged by the works of art for whom it is made. I suppose I shall be censored for living in the past. You cannot change being who and what you are. In a strange way, in varying degrees, no more so than in the writing of these memoirs . . .

'At work in the studio'

Watercolour painting notes, 1950s–80s

25. 'Broad Street in Moonlight', 1961
The textures used throughout the painting help to give a sense of crepuscular light from the moon. The strong diagonals start at the gate and travel up to the roof ridge and down again to the eaves of the second building, before rising towards the shaft of light in the trees. Together with a similar diagonal on the left and an even tonality, these features give a unity and structure to the picture.

26. 'Two Cupids and a Bird', 1973

27. 'The Temple of Venus', 1968
This small panel, one of three, was stolen from the Suffolk Street gallery during delivery and hanging of the exhibition.

28. 'The Temples of Venus'
Repainted after theft of original (**27.** above).

29. RA, 1964
This unique experience is one we shall long remember.

30. 'The Church in Vienne', 1962
The stay in Vienne was long enough to make this drawing. The loose, calligraphic use of line contrast with the strong, dark shapes in the foreground, with the one white square, give interest and vitality.

31. 'The Towers of Darkness', 1964
These medieval towers of darkness had a grim past which is reflected in their massive overpowering domination of the town. The little foreground figures accentuate this, as do the lines of the paved road which helps to emphasise the vertical fortress walls.

32. 'The Haunted House', 1963
The lighting in this picture suggests a stage set for a tragic drama. The wide open shutters in the empty house on the right look rather ghostlike, as does the strongly buttressed tower on the left, guarding the town gate. Two farmers discuss the price of a heifer.

33. 'Sunday Afternoon', 1950
By painting this picture in much lighter tones the drawing and design is accentuated, producing a decorative quality very different from **No. 32**.

34. 'Alsacian Village', 1966
Freely adapted use of architectural elements to create an atmosphere of fantasy, a response induced by several of the

villages visited in Alsace Lorraine. This work is purely decorative. The subject has illuminated space, filling the picture plane vertically.

35. As in **No. 34** all the pictorial material is on the picture plane, hence the flatness. These two villages in the wine-producing area, had a distinctive charming character.

36. 'Charity Farm', 1967
This work in the same group as the preceding picture was bought by Shell and used in their calendar for 1968.

37a. (*Colour plate*). **Stage one.** Taken from sketch book, shows the design arrangement in pencil on board, plus the first application of texture under-painting in acrylic white on the trees.

b. (*Colour plate*). **Stage two.** The picture indicates the use of the under-painting in the trees, right and left of the steps, taken down to water level. Removal of the sluice and first application of colour.

c. (*Colour plate*). **Stage three.** The colour is enriched with the trees left and right, being textured with acrylic white and darkened to give a dramatic light.

d. (*Colour plate*). **Stage four.** The finished watercolour shows the influence of under-painting when colour is again washed over the area, development of the figures and reflections.

38. 'The Donkey Bridge – Minervois', 1987/1988. (*Colour plate*). Another view of the canal with a group of cottages in the distance, under the chateau of Minervois, with the development of the trees and a donkey being led over the bridge.

WATERCOLOUR PAINTING

39. 'Summertime on the Canal du Midi'. (*Colour plate*).
Another aspect of a subject with innumerable possibilities for paintings. Exhibited in 1987 in Bankside Gallery's 'Summer Reflections'.

40. 'The Washing Place', 1981. (*Colour plate*)
In 1981 these washing places were still in common use. They were well organised and equipped for the many women who used them. This was a particularly beautiful place surrounded with a variety of mature trees.

41. 'Fishing by the Lockside', 1976. (*Colour plate*)
A penniche pauses for an overnight stop and owners fish for their next supper. An attempt was made to suggest an early spring-like tranquillity with the avenue of trees in blossom, leading to a distant hamlet.

42. 'The Chapel for the Lock Keepers', 1987. (*Colour plate*)

43. 'The Wave Goodbye', 1979. (*Colour plate*)
A penniche gets underway in evening light. The Chateau shutters close for coming night and the boatman waves goodbye. The large extent of water in the foreground is broken by bridge and chateau reflections.

44. Chateau Biron
This medieval castle, seen from a few miles away along the lower road, was a wonderful sight. The huge mass of its fortification must have been an intimidating problem for any attacking force. It was on our second visit that the chateau site proved to be composed of a number of small buildings of a domestic nature which would once have been occupied by a necessary supporting staff of craftsmen (and women), farmers,

farriers, etc. My painting attempts to harmonise these many varied, architectural elements into a unified whole.

45. Carranac

On our French journeys we had stayed in, or briefly visited, many interesting hamlets, farms and small towns, Carranac being one of the most important. Carranac is divided into two arms by the main road and a hotel (in which we have several times stayed). One arm of the village leads down to the river with some very old timber-framed houses, the other leads to the church, with its splendid sculptural group of entombment, completely unvandalised. The main collection of ancient properties are in this area, with a walk down to the river. The town contains some unique towers, square in plan and quite high; the purpose for which we never had explained. One of these towers can be seen on the left of my painting.

46. Some paintings are grafted, others pruned. The picture in this case was pruned, cut down. The right side was cut off as, after a number of attempts, I could not find a more satisfactory solution. The original drawing is in brown ink and wash. I do not know how I arrived at the colour scheme for this picture, which is so divorced from reality or movement, so it must speak for itself. Quite a number of great works have been cut down, such as the important large painting 'The Connaro family at prayer' by Titian in the National Gallery. The figure on the right has been cut through to reduce the length of the canvas to make it fit over a fireplace! This vandalism is one of the least excusable; but is more common in architecture, where many great buildings have been demolished for convenience or out of ignorance. One of the most regrettable was the largest and most beautiful Abbey complex in Europe: Cluny was demolished to make way for a road (or some such). But we have many examples in the UK which equal this. History records the great number of cities that have been attacked, captured and destroyed by nature and war, from Herculaneum onwards. Recent hurricanes are proof of the devastating destruction which can follow in the wake of earthquakes, or violent wind and sea conditions, combining to produce havoc and misery over very extensive areas of occupation. War does the same, as I saw when living in Berlin in 1946. The enormous devastation demonstrated the awful power of concentrated bombing as we experienced in London.

47. 'The Hermitage Courtyard'
This composite design was planned for development into a more complete painting but in some respects is best left as a drawing.

48.
My war service years were very productive. In many respects my draughtsmanship became mature, more certain of itself. In the very few works I was free to do during my first posting to a gun site in Northern Ireland, the one I illustrated remains. It is of particular interest to me because of its obvious shortcomings. The painting could be extended, continued on either side indefinitely. It has no dominant feature: the trees are all of equal value and appear flat, like pressed leaves, but the feeling of wind and evening rain provide some interest.

49. Chateaux Bonaguil
Paintings are documents of personality which are read by the discerning, who are looking for something more than verisimilitude. One of our journeys in France presented a life lasting vision which has never faded, or in anyway thinned in the passing years. We were on a ridge travelling along a country road with a screen of trees on our right when a sudden

gap revealed the most wonderful view down into the valley. On a rocky eminence stood a huge, dominating castle, which stimulated the imagination through the appreciating eyes and creative power of the mind. The autumn evening atmosphere was soft, warm and balmy with a blue, lingering, distant haze. The vision of a possible realisation of a painting in terms of an organised, structured work of art grew slowly. Fortunately, the sketches I made on the spot were not so specific as to be domineering. Imagination was free to allow a dream to grow, so that things which were not there, gave way to what is there! This metamorphosis does not happen very frequently. I can recall a few pictures which have developed in this way – perhaps my best – but time will judge. I have placed **48** and **49** together to illustrate my thinking.

50. 'Who left the gate open?'
In every respect this is quite a different painting from **49**. From a full orchestra we now have a chamber trio; a visual counterpoint in black, grey and white. The pattern made by a counter-change treatment of the various angles of the surfaces, using one source of light without an atmosphere results in the crisp definition in the drawing. This is offset by the textures which in this painting make the flat surfaces more interesting. There is no movement in the picture, just one suggestion of habitation in the open gate.

51. 'The Old Chalk Pit'
There is a complete contrast from **50**. Light moves through the picture from side to side in broken patches; trees are shedding their leaves with the coming of autumn. The whole area of the picture is tonally agitated by rapid changes in the intensity of the darks and a certain mystery given to the half hidden foreground pond under the trees.

52. 'Farm in Benenden', 1985

The weald, or wold, of Kent still has some lovely fragments remaining of country-life untouched by the spread of the urban nouveau riche. As agriculture declines properties increase, new occupants take the place of the indigenous population. This change has been going on throughout my life, ever since the wonderful 'Haywain' days in my Aunt's thatched cottage which, incidentally, has been completely vandalised by the new owners, doing everything that ignorance can suggest only to increase the property's commercial value.

My picture has no place in reality. It composes a number of buildings based on a pencil sketch made of an entrance to a farm in Benenden. The drawing is suggestive and in no way conclusive. I was left free to create my own imagery, in the dramatic light I found most satisfying, but illuminating, an unreal world. Many of the trees are illogically placed in the painting, but are so arranged to satisfy the demands of creative design, a rearrangement of facts to make a new work of art, as the sun goes down.

53. 'Light on the North Downs Way', 1979. (*Colour plate*)

This little watercolour is purely and simply a statement of light. In writing these notes I have often wondered how these pictures were done because I cannot remember how, or what the compelling motivation was. Every painting is a new creation with no repetition. I cannot now remember ever painting this landscape, but it needs no signature.

54. 'When Evening Comes', 1990

Some of the most enchanting experiences on the canals were the evenings. This time, at the falling day, converted the world into a paradise of silent beauty. Everything in nature spoke a language only heard and understood by the listening spirit.

This painting is the acme of the things most meaningful to me in nature and art. Silence is captivating; it is real as is the dusk of mist for the flight home. The feeling of space from the foreground boat to the bridge and beyond is as convincing as is possible with an invisible horizon, but this helps to enclose the subject within the picture plain. This painting is a miniature biography; it encapsulates the essence of what I am.

55. 'Evening Drinks'

This small painting in gouache, of which there are two, the second in oil on paper, has resulted from the many drawings, made over the years, of people enjoying delightful, social activity with friends, with drinks in the open air.

56. 'Broad Street Farm', 1982

This is another aspect of the Broad Street Farm. The picture is, to a large extent, a rearrangement of the farm buildings. The composition is consolidated by closing-in the surrounding trees and making the tones closely related to the house and distant downland, which in turn fades into the sky. The foreground gates and hedge are also an invention which carries the 'off-white' buildings into the front of the picture but leaving a way through to the house. This was a work, like the one in Philadelphia and others, which was bought by visitors to the studio.

57. 'Bob and Tom, Broad Street Farm', 1987. (*Colour plate*)

When we moved into Broad Street in 1964 there was much that resembled the hamlet as it must have been for centuries. Len Wright, living in Snagbrook House in Hollingbourne, owned a large estate that included Broad Street. Bob Law, Wright's foreman, lived in a small house, Valley View. Tom Eldrett lived in Cedar Bungalow in the lane opposite Broad

Street Farm, and Charlie Chapman lived in Pilgrim's cottage, No. 2. These men all married and lived their lives on the land. By 2006 the inhabitants of this small hamlet, which was once occupied by farmers and craftsmen, will all have gone. The three great barns have also gone, one was demolished and the other two were converted into dwellings. My painting of Broad Street Farm is a composite composition, as so many are. Tom Eldrett's bungalow in now demolished, the only other record of it is in a watercolour of mine now in a private collection. Bob and Tom, small figures on the right, are approaching a pond of my creation.

When Bob retired and moved away Tom remained, working for Peter Horton whose one cow and hens were the only remnants of farming in Broad Street. When Peter died Beryl was on her own (Richard, a solicitor, was in Thurnham, Philippa in Sissinghurst, and Jo in Hollingbourne). This left Tom, who became devoted to Beryl, attending to all her needs and looking after the garden. During the great storm of 1987 lost all our mature lime trees Not only this, but Beryl's splendid tithe barn collapsed, squashing the two cars parked inside. Beryl had two options: to rebuild the barn or sell the site for a new building. After seven years of negotiating with the council, permission was given for the erection of a new building based on the visual appearance of the original structure. So this saw the final demise of Broad Street's three great barns.

58. Scotney Castle

I shall long remember my first visit to Scotney. Having parked the car under the beech trees and entered the National Trust through the turnstile, I found myself on the high ridge overlooking a wide expanse of beautiful park-like countryside. There was a mixture of woodland and meadow reaching to a far distant horizon, so very English. On my right was a plinth which held a piece of sculpture – until recently, when it was stolen. It was a classic figure of high quality. In this eminence one had a splendid view of the castle remains across a lovely garden-like vista, partly man-made. The original castle, surrounded with a moat, now provides a delightful walk giving ever changing aspects of the existing buildings. Little has survived of the medieval castle other than the one machicolated tower, surmounted with a charming lantern. My painting is a combination of several views, as many paintings are. There are a number of drawings of Scotney castle in my sketch books from which I produced two or three versions, now privately owned.

59. The Triptychs: a) 'A Kentish Idyll', b) 'A Dream of Reality'. (*Colour plates*)
During my forty-six years in Brushings Farm House the close association I had with the countryside and the history of the house had, understandably, an affinity with the architecture of Kent. So my outdoor work took me quite naturally to the great houses, castles and domestic buildings in villages and farms. In this particular case, I am referring to Sissinghurst, Scotney and Hever. The extensive number of these drawings suggested that the material could be designed into a larger composition than might be achieved by a number of small pictures, and so the idea grew into 'The Kentish Idyll' triptych.

In some ways, this triptych is just reminiscent of the altar pieces of the Middle Ages. It needed careful selection of the material and thoughtful design that would unite the three sections into a harmonious whole. I thoroughly enjoyed solving this problem by a repetition of similar motives, e.g. a castle is featured at the top of each third section, the wide gates in the centre – like gossamer wings – help to unite the three areas. In the purest sense of the word, the triptychs are not very painterly, but are more closely related to drawing. The areas of colour are strictly controlled by line. The three of them were conceived as designs for large mural decorations which of course never materialised, but the full size cartoons were seen by visitors to the studio and bought.

59c. The Triptychs: 'The French Fantasy'. (*Colour plate*)
From very early times the British Isles have been linked with the movement of peoples across Europe. Many ancient sites in France have their counterparts in Britain, but the land mass in France is so much greater than it is in Britain that many sites are much further apart, which should have contributed to their better preservation. Our journeys in France have been kept well off the beaten track giving us knowledge and experiences of farming and domestic life, which is only obtainable from exploring the countryside well away from city life. The central section reflects one of my main interests, the 'classical tradition', which established standards of excellence in the arts, and which created the principles that established theories based on concepts before 'relativity' or quantum mechanics.

The chief figure is based on a late Greek-Hellenic sculpture with a sympathetic echo of it in the little temple above. Another church-like building bordering the lake leads the eye back to water. The left-hand design is more open – the water from the top flowing down through the arch to the heron in the foreground. These three major designs are not to every man's taste; they are esoteric. They must be looked at and studied to understand their meaning. Why construct pictures that are not easily comprehended? Because most of these easily comprehended productions tend to be commonplace, popular and short-lived, like popular anything. A work without content is superficial, without substance and easily digested.

60. The Camino Antonio Collection, 1988. (These are the most important of ten works).

a. Our bedroom, looking towards the Catalina Mountains.
b. The drawing room with cactus.
c. The dining room, looking onto the terrace.

These three watercolours formed part of the collection of eight paintings, owned by the Chambers family. A larger number of drawings are reproduced in the commemorative book we made for our friend Susan's fiftieth birthday, which is in our possession. The reproductions cover many parts of the now demolished house and broken up estate – records that are of interest to no one.

a. After our first visit in which we were given the guest house, we were thereafter, to occupy a large bedroom in the house, which we enjoyed for the next nine years. My painting shows the window with a panoramic view of the Catalina Mountains of which I made a number of drawings in pen, ink and wash. It was from this window that we saw the side-winder snake, a road runner and a coyote drink from the ceramic bowl let into the sandy soil for them.

A few years ago a mountain lion could be found on the Catalina Mountains, until a man lost his dog and, for some reason, suspicion fell on the lion. So the man, with other neighbours, armed themselves, hunted the solitary creature and shot it. So the environment suffered the loss of a rare and beautiful animal for the sake of one dog. There is no limit to the propagation of the human race; expensive housing with swimming pools (a must), golf courses, or luxurious hotels are all creeping up the mountainside, pushing wildlife back into obscurity. This development is worldwide, and has ominous consequences for the future.

The painting consists of a series of off-white, rectangular shapes. The verticals are repeated in the tall cactus and the only dark is the lamp stand on the windowsill which prevents a drift-out to the left. The colour is quiet and restful, redolent of sleep.

b. & c. The largest area in a house of big rooms was the dining-cum-sitting room. The division was made by a large mahogany cupboard that spanned almost half the width of the room. The larger of the two divisions had the grand piano on which Kim had given a number of recitals for the great pleasure of us all. In addition there were a number of display cabinets, a miscellany of easy-chairs, a handsome tall case-clock, rugs on a tiled floor and a collection of paintings as a result of generous patronage. It was from the two large windows that I made my second and third paintings in this charming commodious room.

The third work shows another view of the desert. The darkest tone reveals how close to the desert trees and cacti will spread if left free from interference, a freedom that encourages wildlife – as we learned, as well as understanding the importance of the terrace walls.

Most days were very hot, the sun shining from a blue, cloudless sky, until the cool of the evening came, when the night-blooming cireus opens its petals to welcome the fertilising moth. It was such a night of quiet stillness when we saw Halley's comet passing miles away, trailing its flaming tail. It was a most mysterious sight as it gradually passed away into space. I thought of it being recorded in the Bayeaux Tapestry, which must have been for the English embroiderers, as great a mystery as the comet is to us even as we have some knowledge of its elliptical orbit around the sun.

'The Farrier's Workshop' (*No picture*)
In one of our expeditions to France we came, quite unexpectedly, to the well fortified towers at the entrance to a small town-cum-village. It was once a flourishing community that is now very much in decline. Across the road, opposite the towers, stood the forge – the most important industry of the past – now vacant. I found it fascinating as I peered through the curtain of mature cobwebs into the abandoned interior where nature had begun to assert itself. Looking through the grimy window panes I found myself prying into the secret life of a farrier, long since dead. His workshop, once the meeting place for farmers and waggoners who sat or stood around chatting whilst smoking their clay pipes as they waited for the shoeing of their horse, now left no sign that they had ever existed. Glancing to the right, to a nail on the door, there hung a much-used leather apron beginning to show the signs of mildew. The tools on the bench lay just as they were put down on their last day of use and the bricks on the floor were outlined in green where ubiquitous grass was beginning to take root. So the place where villagers gathered to talk over the problems of the day now stood empty – a forlorn spectacle of the sad passing of a long history of relatively slow development into one of fast moving technology. As I turned away I could not help thinking of Balzac's novel *Le Pere Goriot* that is redolent with similar feelings of the time.

61. 'A Walk to Paradise Garden'. (*Colour plate*)
The unknown, unrecognised images are often hazy and confused in a dream; others retain a surprising clarity for a long time, sometimes, as with me, a lifetime. The present painting had such a visionary beginning in a wonderful, fleeting dreamlike experience, utterly devoid of any topographical influence – a world of unreality, crystallised into visual form by the manipulation of colour and dramatic tones.

This picture comes nearer than most others in expressing my perception, rather than being a work dominated by subject matter. The works which result from this activating energy are anathema to a generation absorbed in the current aesthetics which now permeate every aspect of society, including dress. This new aesthetic has swept aside the principles of creative design, which have been basic to painting over the last seven hundred years.

62. Oakover Nursery
This work was based on a small sketch which prompted its expansion into its present form.

My paintings may provide glimpses into the past.

63. Brushings Farm House
This small work is taken from a drawing and painted a few years before we left.

64. 'The Swan'

My technical method of under-painting in white acrylic has succeeded in the painting of the trees. Few artists using water-colour based pigments have used a complex number in one work with more freedom than Turner. The light flooding in from the top right increases the value of the darks in the middle and foreground. The people on the bridge make an invisible link with the swan, spanning the space and increasing the feeling of privacy in a secluded place.

65. 'Broad Street Barn'

It was a lucky chance I made the small drawing from which I painted this work. This was a well-constructed building that had been neglected, but which was still useable and could have been adapted to make a splendid studio. However, the opportunity passed and it was bought with the land and promptly demolished by the new owner.

66. 'Broad Street'

67. 'Cedar Bungalow'

I have mentioned this tiny wooden building before. It was Tom Eldrett's home for many years. The sparse hedge was kept in trim, and the small plot had neat rows of vegetable and sweet peas (of which he was very proud). It was the typical kitchen garden of a born country man. But, like the barn, it survives only in my two pictures: **65** and **67**.

68. 'A Late Mooring'

This work forms part of the 'Canal du Midi' series in spite of there being no lock, as in all the others. The steps lead up into a small chateaux garden, intriguing because unseen. The tranquillity of this place was deeply felt, as nature was in no way disturbed by climatic interruptions of wind or rain. Silence reigned over our world as we retired to our bunks.

69. 'The Hen House'

This was a very early painting of the hen house in our first hard winter in Brushings; I eventually rebuilt it to become Eileen's studio. The remains of the cherry tree orchard occupy the middle distance, together with a long line of hedging that was cut down. Behind is the first stage of hedge destruction, which continued for some years, producing enormous fields – one, a mile long, stretched from Hollingbourne half way to Detling.

70. 'The Return to Waldesheere'. (*Colour plate*)

In a warm sunny afternoon in June I was with an inspector colleague motoring along a narrow lane over the Downs, near Dover. My companion was a historian-botanist. We stopped from time to time to pick hedgerow flowers. I remember, on one such occasion when we stopped, I picked up a blue bird's eggshell, but my companion shied away – she being allergic to eggs of every kind. I felt we were motoring along a private road with an interesting termination. I was right because unexpectedly we saw in front of us a splendid eighteenth century mansion. We approached cautiously, even though an uncanny, eerie silence told us that no one was present. The stable block with its clock tower had no horses, grass and small wild flowers were growing between the cobble stones which no longer echoed with the clatter of hooves, and no birds sang to break the silence as we approached through the overgrown garden of grass and weeds the principle wing of the house. To our great surprise, the double doors stood wide open, so we stepped inside into what had been the splendid ballroom of classical proportions and generous decoration of the period. A weird silent submission to sadness, to the inevitable, prevailed – an atmosphere heavy with foreboding which we felt as we walked up the winding stairs to rooms which had architect's drawings upon them in black chalk; these lines indicated where a new door should go, or a fireplace removed. Although no one was there I felt someone was looking at me. We returned to the car. But the experience of the house occupied my mind in many ways, chiefly how to make a painting from the strong reactions arising from our visit, which meant using imaginatively and symbolically the brief information I had in my sketch book. Towards this end I made one or two small pictures in blue and grey before starting on the large work. This painting incorporates three thoughts of a symbolical nature: the 'storied urn' in a restored garden, the weeping willow tree on the bottom right and the minute ghost figure returning home.[1] I wonder what the picture will mean for most people looking at it?

71. 'The Bridge'

It is strange how a small note may keep alive for years an experience half remembered, half forgotten, when, quite suddenly an image vaguely visualised forms the beginning of a painting. I am sure this must be the case in music and poetry where a phrase or a couplet leads on to a sonata or a poem; creativity being an indefinable part of the sensibilities. 'The Bridge' evolved in this way, as did others, all being inventions in an attempt to give form to an emotional echo vibrating from the past.

Light was an invention, a moon-shape repeated by the bridge. The sunset glow suggesting late evening and approaching night.

---

[1] See Thomas Gray's 'Elegy Written in a Country Churchyard': 'Can storied urn or animated bust / Back to its mansion call the fleeting breath?' I understand that permission to convert that house to another use was not granted. So, quite possibly, it has been destroyed by vandals.

72. 'The Marriage at Montmirail'. (*Colour plate*)

There are always a few experiences which dominate a period of travel and exploration. Montmirail – the place and its people – produced one of these unforgettable events. The village was a typical, small French, unexceptional place under the Dentilles – a row of mountain peaks resembling teeth, hence their name. Lunch time in Montmirail, especially on Sundays, as in so many similar villages is a very important hour of the day. After a game of boules, the menfolk return home for the meal all are waiting for. We have seen special items such as roast and cakes being carried home with great care from the communal ovens. This is a special family event, unifying several generations, sitting round one large kitchen table, the conversation being drowned by the clatter of knives and forks.

The hotel in which we stayed was a family-run business, specialising in local events, like marriages, one of which we participated in as invited English visitors. Behind the hotel were quite extensive gardens in which grew a number of ancient horse-chestnut trees. As the wedding breakfast was taking place at twilight, the trees were festooned with fairy lights. When all was set, the table looked wonderful with flowers, glittering wine glasses and decanters, but the most lovely sight was the entry into the garden from the house of the bride, whose white dress and little coronet were quite an ethereal sight and my signal to draw as rapidly as possible in the fading light. It was from these sketches that the painting was done months after our return home.

This work was bought from the Fine Art Society in Bond Street. I remember the Curator from Preston Art Gallery who bought the picture looking at the work for some time and saying 'It is so full of emotion. . . .' Comments of this kind are very rare.

72a. 'The Marriage at Montmirail' – preparatory sketch

73. Albi Cathedral
A powerful, dramatic and large watercolour in dark reds and browns, the monochrome colour scheme emphasises the bulk and weight of the building.

25: *'Broad Street in Moonlight'. Watercolour. 1961. Private Collection, Manchester.*

26: 'Two Cupids and a Bird'
Watercolour. 1973. Private Collection, Portugal.

27:
'The Temple of Venus'
Watercolour. 1968.

28: 'The Temples of Venus'
Watercolour. Repainted after theft of original.

CHANCE FOR *1964* A £10 TRIP

IF any young person between the ages of 18 and 25 wants to go to France on a study tour for £10, they should contact **Mr. W. F. Sheldon** at 12, Ash-

BOTH Mr. Ernest Greenwood and his 21-year-old daughter Dorelia, who live at Brushings Farm House, Broad Street, near Hollingbourne, have exhibits in the summer exhibition at the Royal Academy.

My picture shows one of Mr. Greenwood's paintings.

29: R.A., 1964.

30: 'The Church in Vienne'
Watercolour. 1962. Private Collection.

31: *'The Towers of Darkness'*
Watercolour. 1964. Bristol Education Authority.

32: *'The Haunted House'*
Watercolour. 1963. Private Collection, Bristol.

33: *'Sunday Afternoon'*. Watercolour. 1950. The late Miss Barnes, Private Collection.

34: 'Alsacian Village'
Watercolour. 1966. Collection of City of Sheffield.

35: Alsace Lorraine. Watercolour.

36: 'Charity Farm'. Watercolour. 1967. Purchased by Shell.

*44: **Chateau Biron**. Watercolour.*

*45: **Carranac**. Watercolour.*

46: Watercolour.

47: 'The Hermitage Courtyard'. Watercolour.

48: *Watercolour.*

49: **Chateaux Bonaguil.** *Watercolour.*

50: 'Who left the gate open?'. Watercolour.

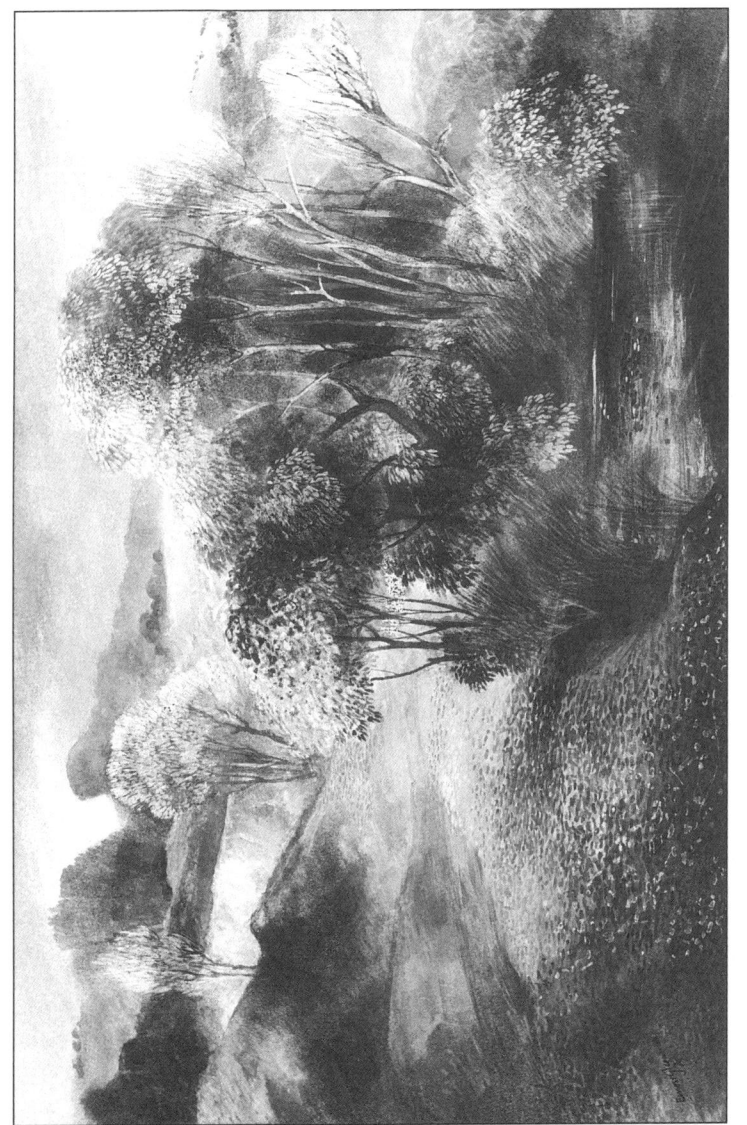

51: 'The Old Chalk Pit'. Watercolour.

52: 'Farm in Benenden'
Watercolour. 1985. Private Collection.

54: 'When Evening Comes'
Watercolour. 1990. Private Collection.

55: 'Evening Drinks'. Watercolour.

56: 'Broad Street Farm'
Watercolour. 1982. Purchased by a Swedish Collector.

58: *Scotney Castle. Watercolour. 1980s. Private Collection.*

a. Our bedroom, looking towards the Catalina Mountains.

b. The drawing room with Cactus.

c. The dining room, looking onto the terrace.

60: *The Camino Antonio Collection. Watercolours.* 1988.

62: Oakover Nursery
Watercolour. Private Collection.

63: Brushings Farm House. Watercolour.

64: *'The Swan'. Watercolour.*

65: 'Broad Street Barn'. Watercolour.

66: 'Broad Street'. Watercolour.

67: *'Cedar Bungalow'. Watercolour.*

68: *'A Late Mooring'. Watercolour.*

69: *'The Hen House'. Watercolour.*

71: *'The Bridge'. Watercolour.*

72a: 'The Marriage at Montmirail'
Preparatory Sketch. 1966.

73: *Albi Cathedral. Watercolour. Collection of Mr & Mrs I. Burrell.*

*37a: Four stages in watercolour painting illustrated
— Stage 1 of 4*

*37b: Four stages in watercolour painting illustrated
— Stage 2 of 4*

*37c: Four stages in watercolour painting illustrated
— Stage 3 of 4*

*37d: Four stages in watercolour painting illustrated
— Stage 4 of 4*

38: *'The Donkey Bridge – Minervois'*
Watercolour. 1987/1988.

39: *'Summertime on the Canal du Midi'*. *Watercolour.*

40: **'The Washing Place', Canal du Midi**
Watercolour. 1981. Private Collection.

41: **'Fishing by the Lockside'**
Watercolour. 1976. Private Collection.

42: *'The Chapel for the Lock Keepers'*
Watercolour. 1987.

43: *'The Wave Goodbye'*
Watercolour. 1979.

53: *'Light on the North Downs Way'*
Watercolour. 1979. Private Collection.

57: *'Bob and Tom, Broad Street Farm'*
Watercolour. 1987. Private Collection.

59a:
The Triptychs:
'A Kentish Idyll'
Watercolour.
Private Collection.

59b: *The Triptychs:*
'A Dream of Reality'
Watercolour.

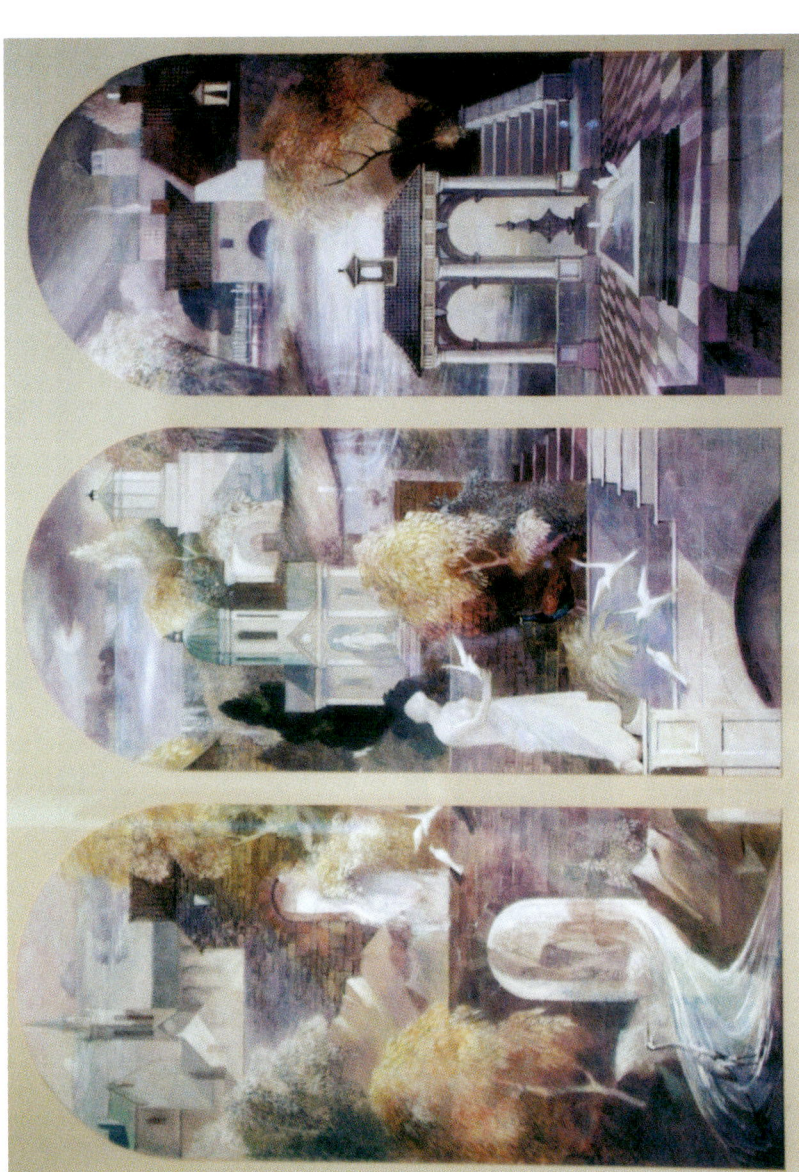

59c:
The Triptychs:
'The French Fantasy'
Watercolour.

61: 'A Walk to Paradise Garden'. Watercolour.

70: 'The Return to Waldersheere'. Watercolour. c1975. Owned by the artist.

72: 'The Marriage at Montmirail'. Watercolour. 1960s. Preston Art Gallery Permanent Collection.

79: *'From Flowers to the Mountains'*
Oil. 1980. Bonhams.

80: *'Spring'*
Oil. Collection of Mr & Mrs Green.

81: *'Autumn'*
Oil. Collection of Mr & Mrs Green.

83: *The late Mrs Freda Chambers*
Oil on canvas. 1995. Private Collection.

82: *Portrait of Mrs Green*
Oil. Private Collection.

85: **'Street Trinity'**
Oil. 1998. Bonhams.

84: **Dr Richard Werden**
Oil on canvas. 1997. Private Collection.

87: *'Young Woman with Pet Cat'*
Oil on canvas. 1943. Bonhams.

86: *Eileen Greenwood*
Oil. 1950s.

III
OIL PAINTING

I HAVE OFTEN WONDERED WHAT THE SUBCONSCIOUS promptings are that makes a young person say 'I want to be a musician' or 'I want to be a painter', even before they know what the work implies. Amongst the remnants of my mother's past there existed part of a mahogany paint box with an unfinished painting of a large bird with a red breast and hooked yellow beak – a cock pheasant, probably. But it was of no interest or value to the family and like so many things, unrecognised and unwanted, found itself in the waste bin. This was my father's paint box and unfinished work – disposed of without any comment or response from mother. I wonder what her thoughts were at seeing the objects which had a long personal history being disposed of. I wonder what will be the fate of my paint box and palette. The past is never completely lost but has to be found again, with curiosity and patience as it was in the case of early man. In a minor way, the secret paint box has stayed locked in my memory for nearly ninety years but is still a powerful image in my mind and makes me think it could have been the source of my wish to be an artist.

During my years at Gravesend School of Art I did not receive a single painting lesson, was not told about brushes or the relative value of those available, nor how to use or handle a palette or the best way of putting out the paint. So to this extent I knew nothing when moving on to the Royal College of Art. The first three terms were spent in the drawing school learning from looking at the work of senior students. Eventually, moving into the painting studios, I was faced with the problem of painting the nude model which was very difficult, yet I was left to fend for myself. I remember Professor Gilbert Spencer (the brother of Stanley) in three years, gave me one unimpressive demonstration. Feeling in need of some guidance with the difficulty, I went to the Principal, Sir William Rothenstien, from whom I received a half-hearted response. This was all the teaching I had in four years. So, in many ways, I was self taught and expected to find my own solutions to present and future problems and prospects, like everyone else.

My painting, mainly still life, was not a direct application of paint with a brush, but rather a move to colour through drawing, a verisimilitude which was, as a result, lacking in fluency. By this time I had become conversant with the various movements which had followed after Cezanne, but few found their way into my thinking to have a positive influence there. The two still life paintings which have only survived in the photographs remind me that the painting of the time was 'tonal'. If I had made a drawing of the vase in charcoal, its shape and bulk would have been shown by the gradation of tone from dark in the shadows to the light side, which was the method I used in the vase and other objects in the group. I had merely used blue paint instead of charcoal. It was this aspect of painting Cezanne changed. Sir William Rothenstien had said in his short lesson 'one surface, one tone', but Cezanne in his work said 'one surface, one colour'. From this statement Cubism was born and has given rise to a number of developments in which colour has taken precedence over every other element, many of which had previously been fused by painters into one composition. This dominance has influenced, together with abstract painting, every department of human interest from T-shirts to advertising. Many T-shirts have taken on the roll of the 'sandwich-board man' in advertising goods and coming events which can be detrimental to human dignity. With hindsight and looking back over the painting I have done since 1940, I can see the dominance drawing has had. I have always enjoyed drawing for its own sake.

Some of the earliest pictures known are the discoveries found at Altamira, in Spain, and in the Dordogne. Neolithic picture symbols were created in secret places and used as a fundamental means of expressing and communicating esoteric thoughts, probably unconsciously, which have haunted mankind in every people who have had a faith and a belief in more than the physical means of survival. These secret ceremonies have resulted in the proliferation of innumerable religions each demanding their individual forms of conformity to a core belief. Such convictions can unite a tribe, a nation or a group of nations influencing their behaviour to one another. Nations with a religion and ceremonial other than their own can, with political motives, rather than altruistic ones, stimulate aggression, suspicion, greed and war; results which we have seen too often in comparatively modern times. There are, however, pleasures from art which require particular sensibilities to enjoy. The philosophy of the beautiful, is not entirely divorced from fashion, but fashion is very ephemeral, as we have recently seen. In dress it can become a uniform, now worn worldwide, to advertise the basic belief in the equality of mankind. Quality transcends fashion, enabling the sensitive and knowledgeable person to differentiate between works of exceptional quality and the mediocre. Mediocrity, the average skill, construction or craft, are characteristic of those works made for general use and, therefore, do not survive as do those of supreme quality, created for a unique national or religious purpose. Such works are treasured and conserved as the masterpieces, in art, architecture, literature and music.

Courtauld stated that art was religion's next of kin. But for many centuries art was the handmaiden of religion. Their kinship, their marriage, was a close relationship in which the artist became the main means whereby education in the Christian faith and history was enhanced. The gradual progressive movement in Europe from the thirteenth to the seventeenth century was dominated by religious pictures. As power moved form pope to prince the subject matter changed automatically and became the way in which the head of state maintained his authority and power. During this period painting changed from being a flat, two dimensional method of working, to a three dimensional one. The rediscovery and development of lineal perspective fascinated a number of painters who spent a great deal of time and energy applying this new science to their paintings. Uccello, in his battle decorations, demonstrates the extent to which he was influenced by his newly acquired knowledge, although the pictures remained decorative. The same can be said of Piero della Francesca who, in his picture of the 'Flagellation' in Urbino, illustrates a similar trend.

Antonio Pollainolo, in his 'Battle of Nude Men', intended to display his knowledge of anatomy but the figures remain flat, the drawing purely lineal, the whole composition two dimensional. By contrast, 'The Last Judgement' by Michelangelo in the Sistine Chapel, reveals a profound understanding of the human figure related to space. Anatomy and dissection were being done not only by Michelangelo but to a greater degree by Leonardo, but by both in secret because the activity was in opposition to the tenets of the Roman Church. The work of dissection must have been a horrible pursuit, especially for Leonardo, who judging by his drawings of the female physiography in detail, such as those in the Royal Collection, must have been drawn with the corpse decomposing rapidly in the hot Italian atmosphere. Stubbs had the same problem to cope with when working on his drawings of the anatomy of the horse.

An understanding of the human form and perspective were only a beginning of what the new sciences had to teach painters. They quickly saw a new pictorial opportunity, seeing how objects with distance decreased in size, made so by atmospheric conditions. With the development of an interest in landscape, atmosphere took on a new significance since light and space became a new departure in themselves, eventually leading to a study of colour, as in the paintings of haystacks by Monet. The use of paint has also changed dramatically since Michelangelo painted the Holy Family. This work was essentially the product of a sculptor, being almost monochromatic. Painting preceeding this, whether on panel or wall (as in fresco) was done in watercolour. By the turn of the sixteenth century the use of oil paint had begun to filter through from Flanders. The religious pictures painted often had a basic design based on a box-like interior, in which a window or two looked out onto a town or landscape in which little figures or horsemen produced an element of scale and space – a device even used by Leonardo. Titian in Venice made a positive and permanent change in the use of pigments, which, with brushwork, colour and tonality, constitute the hallmark of a great artist.

With Rembrandt, chiaroscuro reached the highest and most meaningful use of tone (shadows) that have ever been painted. The immediate environment in which a figure is surrounded is not just a background, but a dimly lit but luminous and mysterious space with an indefinable depth. This profound use of paint has only to be set against Franz Hals to have the difference emphasised. By contrast, Rubens and Gainsborough have used the medium like watercolour but, with the advent of post-Impressionism another major change has taken place with the manipulation and break up of the painted surface in which subject matter almost disappears as in some of the work of Vuillard.

My painting saw many phases before any clear direction became apparent. I produced a few paintings in oil on canvas, experimenting with Cubism (the only surviving example of this is now with Bonhams), but it only showed that this degree of abstraction was not for me. Living twenty five years in the Darenth Valley at Otford, near Shoreham, had a far greater influence than I was then conscious of. It was rather the poetic romanticism of Palmer which had a strange, subconscious link with my boyhood experience of the Haywain and the mysticism of William Blake's verse which shaped my future.

What you are in the beginning is how you remain throughout life. My earliest experiences were concerned with the countryside in all weathers, in walking and cycling. Walking, as I have said elsewhere, was an absolute necessity and a great pleasure; fatigue after a long walk really was a satisfying pleasure. Walking in all weathers made me keenly conscious of the seasons which were then clearly defined. There were summer nights which were so hot my two brothers and I slept in the garden. On these few days in the year, lying awake, looking into the sky, with the stars and moon illuminating the night that the mystery of the universe was apprehended. It was on one of these nights, watching the moon rise slowly and majestically, that it became a lasting symbol of tranquillity for me.

I have mentioned this infatuation before – the moon in all its phases has featured in many of my paintings for people to notice, comment and joke about, good-naturedly, of course. I am sorry this wonderful phenomenon has been soiled with the feet of human beings. Nevertheless, it has contributed, or even been the seed from which a love and respect for nature has grown and has finally brought a certain unity to my painting, but it took a long time. After my release from the armed forces I was in a turmoil of indecision about what sort of painter I wished to be.

The visual memory is sharpened and becomes more accurate when, year after year, one continues drawing and painting simply because it is impossible to look and paint simultaneously. Looking back on drawings and paintings made years ago they jump into focus when prompted by the writing of these memoirs, bringing into view again things long-thought forgotten. It was not until after Michelangelo that the nude female was used in painting in a non-religious context (his women were adapted from male models, like other painters of the period). Giorgione's 'Sleeping Venus' now in Dresden is probably the earliest use of a female model. There are, however, comparatively few painters, among a total of many hundreds, who have painted the nude female exclusively, or as part of a complex composition; Titian, Rubens, Rembrandt and Renoir are four outstanding masters who have done both. Manet's 'Olympia' stands alone. My painting 'A girl wearing a turban with a black cat on her lap' is only partially nude, but I spent many sittings on a work which I think was good for its time and, when the fashion changes, probably for a long time.

Shortly after moving to Bridge Cottage I needed a space to paint in – a room where a work in progress could be left in safety. In Otford at that time (the 1950s), there were all the individually owned businesses that were always associated with similar village communities in England. Apart from a small builders office and yard owned by John Nash, the next in size was a substantial hardware store. There were two butchers, a baker, greengrocer, a haberdashery owned by an elderly lady (even then old fashioned, but delightful) and a barber's shop. Bill Jeffrey, the barber, had a small room above his shop that was to become my studio until we left to move into Brushings Farmhouse in 1960. Bill, living on his own in his small, one man business, was a 'throw back' in time. The shop window was very seldom cleaned and was an undisturbed haven for flies amongst packet of faded foreign stamps, a few tins of ointment covered in dust and a notice saying 'umbrellas repaired'. The woodwork had long since given up the pretence of ever having been painted. The floor was covered by a much worn and very cheap linoleum. The barber's chair, second-hand by its appearance, was, apart from a few chairs for waiting customers (seldom needed), placed at right angle to an ancient, coal-heated stove on which Bill did his cooking, or boiled a kettle to make a cup of tea. He announced one morning he thought he would make for himself a 'stoo'! He was a guileless man. I only patronised his hair cutting skill once. His work was quite good but the cloth he put round my neck was the most dirty, the most unhygienic I had ever seen, so I left his haircutting skills for others, confining my visits to my studio upstairs.

Before I could begin work it was necessary to clear away a small pile of rotting seed potatoes, otherwise it conformed to the layman's idea of an artist's studio in the garret, perfectly complete with old whitewash peeling from the ceiling, as downstairs. It was in this room that I painted my portrait of the 'Dancer Resting'. It was my only full-length portrait as circumstances did not provide another opportunity. This painting showed quite a different technical approach from that used in the work 'Girl with a turban and black cat on her lap'. The Dancer was almost monochromatic in treatment. Shown in the

R.A. Summer Exhibition it received a good write-up but nothing more. The painting is now with Bonhams.

'From Bridge Cottage window': This long panel was related to the proportions of the window through which the garden and cottages beyond made an interesting, familiar background, in contrast to the spring flowers on the window sill. This painting had a sad end. A doctor friend seeing the work asked if he could borrow it to decorate a wall in his surgery. I agreed to this on a short-term basis, but as the short-term passed into a long-term, I asked for its return only to learn that it had been shown for a short period only and was now stored in his coal shed! On its return to me, my painting was filthy with coal dust and dirt and, as a result, cut into three, so unfortunately now only a good photograph exists. This was not the first time that my painting had been ignominiously treated. The most destructive was, of course, the Chislehurst cycle.

The 'Coopers' decorations 1950–1956 (Pictures not reproduced in this volume)

Drawing continued to be my chief occupation and interest before and during the war years, chiefly in the field of portraiture. It was not until 1950 that I had the chance to work on the 'Coopers' project. Until then I had used oil paint, applying it to the canvas quite thickly with medium size hog-hair brushes. Before I started work on the first panel I tried out the paint and decided on a thin application to obtain the maximum help from a brilliant, ivory-like ground.

No. 1. Opposite the entrance to the park and across the lane was a small chapel. I used this as my first subject and painted two women leaving the chapel garden, suggesting the two Marys. This was the smallest of the sixteen panels and was a convenient way of testing the painted surfaces.

No. 2. 'Disputation'
Most of the figures in this panel were drawn from the young women during rehearsals. These groups were designed on a variety of different levels which the steps provided. This arrangement was necessary as the format was a tall and narrow rectangle. The brick wall running through all the panels formed a link with each one of them.

No. 3. 'Noah receiving the return of the dove'
This was a particularly interesting section to work on because it contained an element of a small industry, exclusive to Otford. A certain Mr Rogers lived in what is the most ancient medieval timber framed house in the village, which in times past was probably lived in by a wealthy merchant or lord of the manor. It is a large building, rich in timberwork, both inside and out. The generously proportioned hall has a gallery at one end. Mr Rogers employed Mr and Mrs Kilbey as gardener and housekeeper respectively. They had two children of Dorelia's age, a boy and a girl, who often played together after school. Behind the house Mr Rogers owned a meadow that was kept damp and sometimes wet by the river Darenth. There he grew willow trees for the manufacture of cricket bats. I used this small plantation in No. 3 as the vertical trees and Noah's slender figure fitted the shape of the panel very well. I particularly enjoyed painting this section as it commemorated twenty-five happy years in Otford.

No. 4. 'The Nativity'
It was not easy to find another image of this age-old subject of 'mother and child' which through the centuries had been used as a symbol of the sacrosanct nature of parenthood.

No. 5. 'Angels of the annunciation'
The annunciation of this prophetic message was a particularly important subject, especially from the fourteenth to seventeenth centuries in Italy. It formed the essential beginning of the life of Christ. The earliest of the young Leonardo's paintings was of this subject when working as an apprentice to Andrea del Veroccio.

No. 6. 'The Flight into Egypt'
The wide lane leading up to Colonel Edleman's house (he was the original owner of Coopers), the family home – which has since been demolished to make room for yet more houses – terminates the road up to which plod the two little figures representing Mary and Joseph. I hoped that the relatively empty space would balance the previous two, the format being well-filled with incident. I know that some panels may not in themselves be particularly interesting, largely because of the absence of any dramatic chiascuro but the small intimate size of the room only required an even tonality.

Nos. 7 and 8. This was a small area in the corner of the room, almost matching the space on the right angle on the window side. On the smaller of the two I painted 'The Firmament', and on the larger one, 'The

Crucifixion'. Both were mutilated in the demolition, and destroyed.

No. 9. 'The two Marys with the winding sheet'
This was accentuated by placing the figures well back in the format and bringing the winding sheet to the bottom of the picture. As this was part of the cycle which occupied a space between the windows it needed larger figures and a broader treatment. With hindsight I could have been more imaginative in the treatment of the wall behind the two women (e.g. as a brick sepulchre). It is for this reason that some pictures take a long time to coalesce and there are times when they never do, when pictures remain unfinished.

No. 10. 'Three Kings with a sleeping gardener'
In this painting the wall theme is treated with greater variety. In the far distance a horseman is seen approaching the garden.

No. 11. 'The Cloister'
The two monks writing in a cloister represent the church composing the tenets which were intended to be the rules governing every aspect of human behaviour and duties to God. To a certain extent these commands governed the lives of Christians until the rise of the Spanish Inquisition (the tribunal established in 1232 to 1820 to preserve the supremacy of the Roman Catholics in Europe by suppressing heresy, notably in Spain), the tyranny and prohibition of free thinking upon which Goya made his bitter attack.

No. 12. The meeting of David and Solomon.

No. 13. 'Distant view of Coopers'
The one landscape of the house and tree of Lebanon fitted into the rectangular panel over the fireplace. It was intended to provide an aspect of the house showing where the paintings were once to be seen.

No. 14. This corner was an awkward narrow panel on which I painted a fence, a perch for a variety of local birds. This small section was never seen after demolition.

No. 15. 'The Expulsion'
The cloak of evil has fallen over Adam. The rocky landscape was taken from a sketch book study, as was the gate. The spade and rake symbolise the toil to come. In the foreground, the flowers in the garden they were leaving. Adam, like a blind man, had missed the open gate leading to the inhospitable land outside. This section has more symbolism than most and reminds me of a statement by Ngaio Marsh which reads 'We deprive ourselves aesthetically when we forego the advantages of symbolism'. I know that the individual panels may not in themselves be particularly interesting, but I hoped that in the completed work they would produce an original statement of the painter's intent.

The Tucson experience

All our extensive travelling on cruise ships had been done over the past fifteen years in Europe, India and the Far East. These memorable years had acquainted us with many historic sites and the associated museum collections. The long history from Neolithic to Classical Hellenist and Roman times was for us a most interesting enriching experience. It was a keen pursuit of knowledge and friendship that made the art group a delight to work with, especially when they sorted themselves in threes and fours on a project with a leader. It was under these conditions that our first contact with Freda (a leader) and Susan took place, which led to a long-lasting friendship. Camino Antonio, their home in Tucson, was situated in twenty five acres of what, though it was described as desert, was in fact the habitat of many animals and plants that were new to us. One of the most mysterious was the night flowering cactus, which only opens its petals when a certain night-flying moth approaches. It then opens up to allow the moth to fertilise the flower. We stayed up some nights to watch this astonishing phenomenon take place in Freda's garden, in moonlight, which enhanced the experience.

Another remarkable plant we saw is the giant cactus, the saquara, which grows to a height of fifteen to twenty feet or more, and after heavy rain it can weigh several tons. This cactus is only to be seen in Arizona where it is very prolific, growing quite extensively on the hillsides. My sketchbook of drawings made from the boundary walk in Freda's garden contains the skeleton of one of these plants.

Our ten visits to Tucson as guests of the Chambers were remarkable in many ways. Freda had three children: two sons and a daughter, Susan. Freda's husband and one son had died, just leaving Freda and Susan living in a large property. We first met these two women as members of our art group on a Swan Hellenic cruise when Eileen and I were working as guest lecturers. Freda had had professional training in a European art school, but at which one I never knew. She was a very competent painter, especially in the way she handled thick paint with confidence, unifying all the elements of the subject matter as a post-Impressionist. Her pictures tended to be flat objects remaining on the picture plane with no aerial perspective or atmosphere, but were very personal, interesting, and arresting in vitality. She was very gentle and generous – a face full of experiences, mainly of sadness and disappointment. Freda's husband, a geologist, died shortly before we met, and her son by an accident, but of these events Freda never spoke. In ten years she never once mentioned her husband, Arthur, but I gathered from scraps of information that he was quite unlovable in every sense – selfish in the extreme. We suspect, with no evidence, that he could have been the cause of Susan's illness. My portraits of Freda may reflect some of these hidden facts. Susan suffered from anorexia and was painfully thin when we first met her on the ship. She had a brilliant mind, obtaining a Masters Degree in Japanese and therefore having a special interest in the art and craft of that country. In spite of her illness she had enormous energy. On the ship she walked and walked. At home, Susan had innumerable interests; she played duets with a friend on their grand piano and cut stencils for the screen printing she used for decorating garments which she made for children and adults, with some assistance from her great friend Debbi. Susan's compulsive activities began in the early morning with a long walk, often reading as she went. She spent time once or twice a week, nine-pin bowling, square dancing, helping to establish a women's craft centre, or making watercolour drawings of plants which she had printed as cards for a charity. She patronised the arts, buying works of all sorts that covered the walls of her bedroom and house. Generally, it was a kind of frenzied activity which her ailing body could not maintain indefinitely; as Debbi said to her once '. . . you must put on some weight. If you fall ill you just won't make it . . .' How right she was.

One of the most interesting features of life in Tucson was the Gas Light Theatre which staged Edwardian melodrama shows. These productions were introduced by a non-stop pianist to lead the audience in singing popular songs of the period while tucking into free bowls of popcorn, just as a preliminary to the large meals offered for consumption ordered during the interval. The arrival of two English visitors had been passed on to the manager who, after making the announcement, led the audience with cheers and clapping, but no boos!

It was at one such performance that we first met Art, being a friend of the Chambers'. He was a frequent member of the numerous dinner parties Susan provided for her many friends. As time passed Art became a more frequent visitor to Camino Antonio. These were the days when we saw a positive decline in Freda's health – she needed constant attention which is where Art proved to be a wonderful friend and nurse. Freda's surviving son, Wid, bought himself a bungalow one thousand miles from Tucson, paying intermittent visits to Freda. Susan sought elsewhere for companionship. This may have been one of the factors which resulted in frequent dinner parties. Art was always one of the guests and saw quite clearly how the two women were living, in their large house. His courtship and marriage to Susan were the eventual happy outcome for Susan, who was in such need for companionship and the security this gave.

So Susan and Art made their second visit to Brushings in the summer of 1997. The flight had upset Susan, necessitating help at Heathrow. As soon as we saw her we could see how ill she was and so she went straight to bed, and the day afterwards Art made arrangements for their return home where, a few days afterwards, she died. This was a blessing because, had she lived, she would have been an invalid, a condition she could not have tolerated. It was very extraordinary that Susan all but died in our house. She was a wonderful person, unique in so many ways, mostly in affectionate consideration for others. I never heard her say a word of criticism or unkindness about anybody. On each of our visits it was her pleasure to give us a special treat – arranging for our flights into Mexico, the Grand Canyon, Monument Valley, Petrified Forest, journeys to Phoenix, Benson and innumerable places of historic and geological interest as well as the ghost towns and the chain of Catholic missions starting in Mexico and ending in Tucson at St. Xavier. Art is now happily remarried, making a pair for whom we have a great affection. With the death of Freda and Susan our long association with the Chambers came to an end dramatically with the complete demolition of Camino Antonio. It also ended a very eventful period of educational exploration and creative work of our own.

Portraiture

The portrait and its history can be a key factor in any investigation into the political or religious development of a country. It established the hierarchy in the military field, it identifies individuals and their position in national administration. It distinguishes the great innovators in the sciences and the arts, it separates men and women of distinction. In Egypt, portraits in stone have been used for dating purposes, covering thousands of years, until encaustic painting took its place. The most remarkable surviving examples found at Faiyum were of the early centuries AD. The portrait in Roman times was limited to the Emperor and a small numbers of the aristocracy, but the early years of the Italian Renaissance saw a revival of this genre. The collecting of Hellenistic and Roman objects, especially of jewellery and cameos, resulted in the profile portrait, of which two examples are Domenico Veneziano's

'Portrait of a Lady' and Piero della Francesca's portraits of 'Federico da Montefeltro and his wife'. This form of portraiture has survived in modern coinage. Portrait painting in Europe, first in France and then in England, was used to promote and stabilise an aristocratic society. The great painters in this category are many, but Holbein and Van Dyke were supreme masters. This form of aggrandisement continued until the invention and development of photography – now the 'media'. This form of persuasion emphasises the importance of government, and a multiplicity of commercial products being pushed into prominence to serve the interest of a new, money-bred aristocracy.

Oil Painting notes

74. 1940s: Votty Bach

The Votty Bach years were wonderful in many ways. Most of my work done in those visits, in all seasons, have gone. I do not think of the several portraits, and the landscapes a single canvas remains. All were sold. The two paintings reproduced give an idea of my approach to the recording of the mountainous countryside, continually changing under the shadows of passing clouds. My one painting, done while standing in the snow was bought. The owner sold it to The Fine Art Society in Bond Street where, some years later, I saw it prominently displayed. Living in our Welsh cottage brought us as close to nature and to country people as we are ever likely to be again.

75. 1940: 'The Neglected Garden'

This is as much a flower painting as it is a landscape. The angle of the sheet of corrugated iron echoes the light on the wall, both of which close-in the foreground, which helps to give space to the hills beyond.

76. 1951: 'Flowers by the Window'
Although painted some years later, this work is closely related to 'The Neglected Garden'; both being essentially flower paintings of similar plants. This was painted from our sitting-room-cum-kitchen at Votty Bach.

77. 1950: A study for 'The Planets'
For some years I had enjoyed the orchestral music of Holst but the series of oil paintings based on my interpretation was never completed. The painting 'Neptune' was the only one finished to my satisfaction, now privately owned. Studies for Venus are with Bonhams, to mystify everyone! The other part of the series illustrated here is not quite finished as some of the standing pillars were intended to be slightly changed into figures. But it is complete as it is, free to speak its own language.

78. 1962: 'The Black Gondola'
This unique city, Venice, is remarkable; being the only one to survive of several cities built on or around a network of canals. Venice is a rich depository of works of art attracting thousands of visitors during the summer for centuries. It has been a major goal for travellers, who have increased enormously as easy, rapid transport has facilitated the development of world travel. The varied and many channels of the media throughout the world have given the peoples of the earth every aspect of Venice in every season. This familiarity has made it difficult to find a new and personal image from the thousands that have been produced, from the seventeenth century onwards. I, therefore, chose one object to form the subject of this work. I thought it would make a suitable symbol for a city with an inexhaustible charm.

79. 1980: 'From Flowers to the Mountains'. (*Colour plate*)
This picture was painted years after the briefest pencil sketch was made. It is impossible to say precisely why the original impulse to record the experience took so long. I must have been working on other things but the 'Flowers to the Mountain' idea finally materialised into a new picture.

80. Flower painting: **'Spring'.** (*Colour plate*)

81. Flower painting: **'Autumn'.** (*Colour plate*)

82. Portrait of Mrs Green. (*Colour plate*)

83. The late Mrs Freda Chambers. (*Colour plate*)

84. Dr Richard Werden. (*Colour plate*)

85. 1998: 'Street Trinity'. (*Colour plate*)
The late evening glow and a rising mist is reducing the sharpness and clarity of the moon in the falling light of passing day.

86. Eileen Greenwood, 1950s. (*Colour plate*)

87. 'Young Woman with Pet Cat'. (*Colour plate*)

*74: **The Welsh Hills from Votty Bach***
Oil on canvas. 1940.

75: 'The Neglected Garden'
Oil on canvas. 1940. Private Collection.

76: *'Flowers by the Window'*
Oil on canvas. 1951. Private Collection.

77: *A study for 'The Planets'*
Oil. 1950.

78: *'The Black Gondola'*
Oil on canvas. 1962. Private Collection.

IV

THE DRAWINGS

THE EARLIEST INDICATIONS OF MAN'S EXISTENCE in the world are recorded in caves and on rock faces in many countries in places which seem to have had a particular significance to the peoples by and for whom they were made. From then on, the means of drawing as a means of communication has become a form of speech with an enormous vocabulary, identifying individual artists and writers with their country of origin so clearly that we can at once recognise a Rembrandt from a work by a scribe in China. Many Neolithic and earlier peoples have recorded in their drawings, incidents of historical interest for those whose knowledge can interpret the symbols; but as time passed and people settled into larger organised communities, individuals with a special aptitude in graphic skills gradually became of great value to the village or town that employed them in every way. These scribes became indispensable in matters of jurisprudence, in peace time, and in war. So, the calligraphic skills became separated by the type of use to which the artist could employ them. Gradually, the number of tools used to make lines was increased and because a particular tool produces a characteristic mark or line, the infinite possibilities were immediately put into use by innovative artists. So, pencil, silver point, pen, charcoal and chalk were some of the means by which draughtsmen extended their power of expression as indicated in my simple analysis in some of the sketch book drawings. But it is much better to look at Leonardo's cartoon, a drawing by Ingres, or Rembrandt, to clarify this observation.

Ideas are often expressed in rapid, powerfully-made drawings. As the artist's idea develops so do the numbers of drawings and studies which map the path towards the completion of a painting. Quite often, paintings are lost or destroyed, and are only known by the surviving studies. There have been collectors through the centuries who have specialised in drawings and prints, of whom Vasari (1450) was one of the pioneers. Vasari made a collection of drawings obtained from the great artists of his time, including Michelangelo, who was a great friend of his. Vasari's acquisition is frequently mentioned in his writings. Unfortunately, the book — or folio — was subsequently broken up and lost. My few drawings, reproduced here, are a selection from about five hundred, now in the keeping of my grandson, Russell. These are supplemented by one thousand five hundred or so in the sketch books, many of them made for the enjoyment that drawing brings, a pleasure that is typified by the following studies.

Notes to the Drawings

88. The earliest of all the drawings in a dry-point drawing of myself, made in 1935. This is the only print from the plate to survive.

89. All 1936.

a. A stabled horse. Pen and wash.

b. A stabled carthorse. Pen and blue wash.

c. Study of a cow. Pen and blue wash.

90. This drawing was made in Berlin, during my time in the Rehabilitation Centre which quite probably contained the only concert grand piano in the ruined city. The instrument was used without consent on a regular basis by a young pianist. She was no beginner, and listening to her practising a certain Beethoven sonata gave me great pleasure. I made several drawings of her, and the one I framed – the one I thought the most successful for its expression of her sensitivity – is now owned by an American pianist Dr. K. Hayashi.

91. A drawing of my mother.

Landscape (No picture)
I have used this form of design in a much larger picture where the maximum amount of landscape was achieved by a very high horizon almost as though the picture was painted on a flat plain and not one in which perspective is used to obtain space in depth. This picture is stabilised and revolves around the central trees, in contrast to 'Street Trinity'.

92a, b, c, & d: Four monochromatic drawings
These four works with others form a group developed since the move from Brushings to Lakeside. The lack of all facilities resulted in a return to the sketch books for material and motivation. The creating of this series of ten composite works has provided a way of using sketch book drawings to produce a number of imaginative compositions. These three drawings and one watercolour (**92c**) were conceived in their present form

as drawings, that is, the dominance of the line is sacrosanct with the areas of tone chosen to produce an interesting counterchange of pattern of light and dark. The drawing is as precise as I could make it; it is a series I very much enjoyed.

93. 'The Man with a Pipe'
This was made during one of our trips to Graz in Austria in the 1940s.

94. 'Bridge Cottage'
This pencil drawing, heightened with white, shows the back of the house with Dorelia's tent, and Rufus – asleep. This is very much a factual study, a reminder of the twenty-five formative years in which we lived in the house.

95. 'The Smiling Girl'
One of my more satisfactory studies. I think this drawing must speak for itself.

96a, b, c, & d: Dorelia
Four pencil drawings of Dorelia.

97.
This drawing of the sitter was designed to fit the long rectangular format emphasised by the area of black running diagonally from bottom right. The brush line makes a dramatic foil to the dark shape.

98a & b. Varied media.

99.
Portrait of a young woman from Ripon. About 1940.

100.
This interesting drawing of the late Slim who began life as an actor then suddenly gave up and went to Burma, joined

the police and then was murdered. This work was done during the war on one of my leaves.

101. A character study of an employee of ours whom we found unreliable but a patient sitter.

102. Our short-term friend, Peter, escaped from a prison in Germany and became an interpreter in the British Army. The wire fence pattern suggests the prison from which he escaped in 1943.

103. 'A British Soldier', 1945.

104. 'The Garden Party'
During the many times we went ashore with our art groups we frequently paused for refreshment; this gave an opportunity to study and draw local people and holiday makers. Time was usually limited by the timetable, but we managed to make many rapid studies of people, singly or in groups. 'The Garden Party' was the result of such observations. The composing process: the movement of the figures reveals their focus upon a comment being made by the waiter causing their heads to turn to the left, while their bodies all lean inwards, forms the front of the picture plain. Their heads making a great loop enclosing the two smaller people. Analysis could go further, but I think this will suffice to explain the process of thought during the development of the drawing to its final stage.

105. 'A Suffolk Mill'
This drawing was made from the need to record a fascinating building almost as a form of industrial archaeology. But this group of buildings held an indefinable appeal – romantic and aesthetic, speaking so clearly of a busy industry serving the

needs of a local population, an industry in which most of the villagers were involved in one way or another. Work was of a different kind from that of the twentieth century. Then it was the means by which individuals made a personal contribution towards a known end. The tools to a large extent were their own hands. The tools now have grown into gigantic machines.

But the artist has sensibilities which are particularly attuned to an awareness of the subtleties of nature's presence. The smell of the mill pond and water in the slow moving river, the wild flowers and water plants, the very air we breathe, help to enrich the gift of life.

French village, Serenaque. (No picture)
A small town or village built dramatically on the edge of a deep cliff. The castle occupied the summit overlooking an extensive panoramic view of the plain below. The rear of the town was fortified with massive walls and strong gates. The town inside had an atmosphere of quiet exclusiveness, with a generous square, essential for market days or for the assembling of troops in war times. On the day of my visit, the square was empty except for a few gossiping women with their children. It gave a strong impression that nothing had changed for a long time.

106 & 107: The French Villages
There are many little towns in rural France that can be found well away form large towns and cities, tourist routes, and motorways which are a fascinating survival of life in past times. The motor roads, linking the large cities and seaside resorts, take the shortest distance – a straight line – as the Romans knew so well. The auto-routes designed on the same principle have left areas of the country unmolested. Until recently, villagers did very little travelling, except upon

winding narrow roads, to visit neighbours or a nearby town. Many of these small towns have an interesting past; most have grown up round a castle, on the pilgrim routes or have been established as Bastides. Some villages grew and developed slowly, or not at all and so remained the same for decades. Some indication of this is seen in many houses which have a ground floor or basement entrance on street level. Such spaces provided excellent and safe accommodation for goats, sheep, and sometimes cows or horses. As farming and domestic life change, many of the old practices changed too, but we have seen during our past journeys, examples of these close relationships of people with animals, nature, the land, and the satisfaction it gave, as just once, and only once, did I see a farmer plough with a team of oxen.

108. The Hermitage Courtyard

109. 'Evening Bonfire'

110. Woodcuts, Etching and Engraving

On returning from the British School in Rome to the Royal College of Art I moved into the School of Etching and Engraving. Only now, looking back, I realise how one-sided was the curriculum there. The two instructors were excellent artists/craftsmen with high reputations; but their curriculum was deficient in so far as no lectures were organised covering the history of etching and associated crafts. I would have welcomed lectures especially as I now know woodcuts were probably the beginning of many, very different, crafts.

Woodcuts: Woodcuts were made by cutting grooves into a flat block with chisels and knives in order to make an image, pattern or picture. Any caption cut into the same surface had to be done backwards because any printing automatically reversed. When pictures and captions were printed on one sheet and then bound they formed what is called a 'block book'. These were in production by 1430, but this form died out by about 1480 with the invention of moveable type, which could be reused. This method of printing was in direct contrast to intaglio etching.

Etching: If an image or groove was cut into a woodblock it automatically 'printed' white, but if a scratch or hatching was made in a zinc or copper plate, this, when filled with ink and put under pressure printed black. The prints produced by Dürer are great examples of a genius perfecting a technical process from its infancy to a method used today. So, when I made my etchings, I was using a method hundreds of years old.

The illustrated etchings of mine, two portraits and two landscapes, were very early attempts to understand and use a draughtsman's tool with imagination. The illustrations for two of Thomas Hardy's novels were never finished; a process of burnishing and scraping to produce high and medium light areas was never done. The portraits show the influence of Rembrandt, especially in the case of the woman wearing a soft hat. The two landscapes were drawn into a soft wax ground on the site. I carried the copper plates on my back in a haversack, the subsequent prints are not very good but introduced me to a way of working out of doors.

Engraving: Engraving is related to etching but, whereas the groove to hold printing ink is etched in the copper plate with acid, the engraved line is made with a burin being pushed over the surface to produce a line similar to a plough leaving a furrow, which automatically holds ink. The burin passing over the surface throws up a burr on each side, which also holds ink, widening the ultimate black line. This can be controlled by scraping away the burr totally or in part.

My only existing engraving is a self-portrait owned by a grandson.

88: Self-portrait
Dry-point drawing. 1935.

89a: A Stabled Horse
Pen & Wash. 1936.

89b: A Stabled Carthorse
Pen & Wash. 1936. Private Collection.

89c: Study of a Cow
Pen & Wash. 1936. Private Collection.

90: Pianist in Berlin

91: *My Mother*

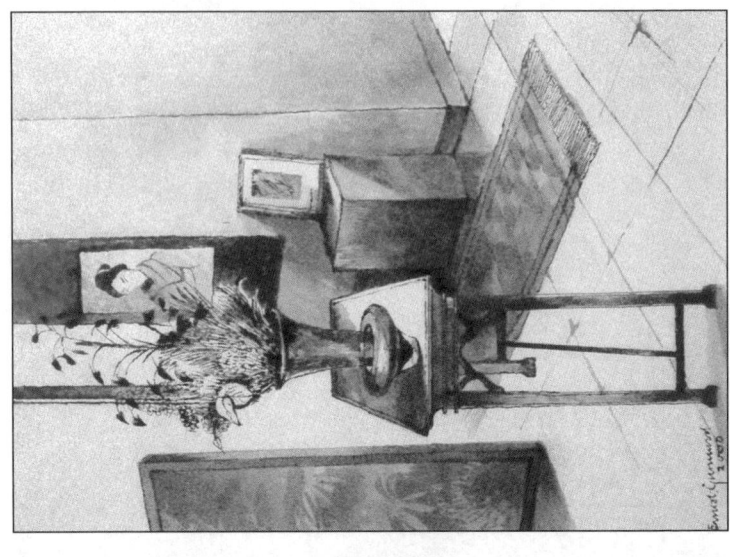
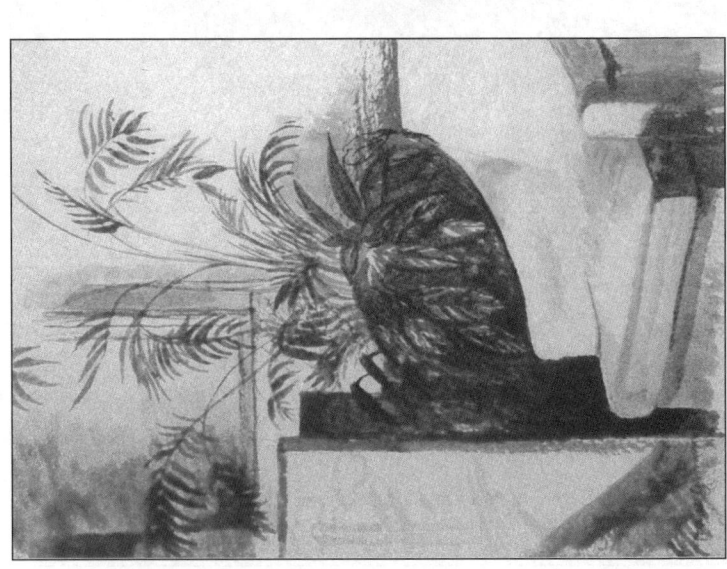

92 a & b: Monochromatic drawings

92 c & d: Monochromatic drawings

93: 'The Man with a Pipe'

94: 'Bridge Cottage'

95: *'The Smiling Girl'*
Pencil. 1944. Private Collection.

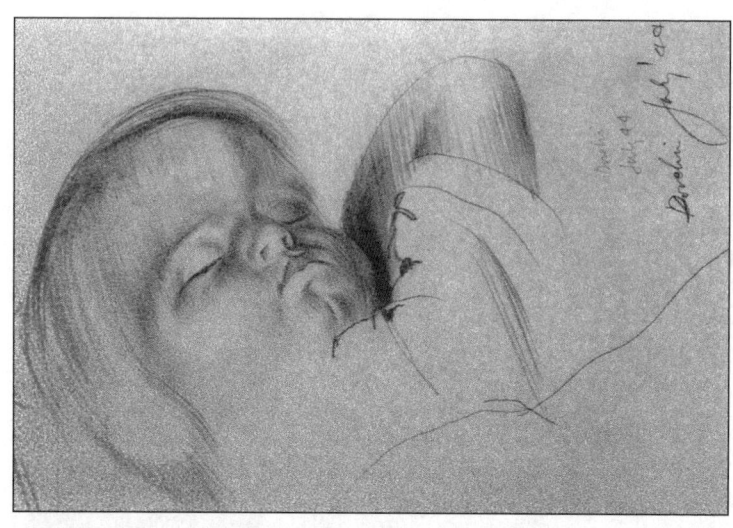

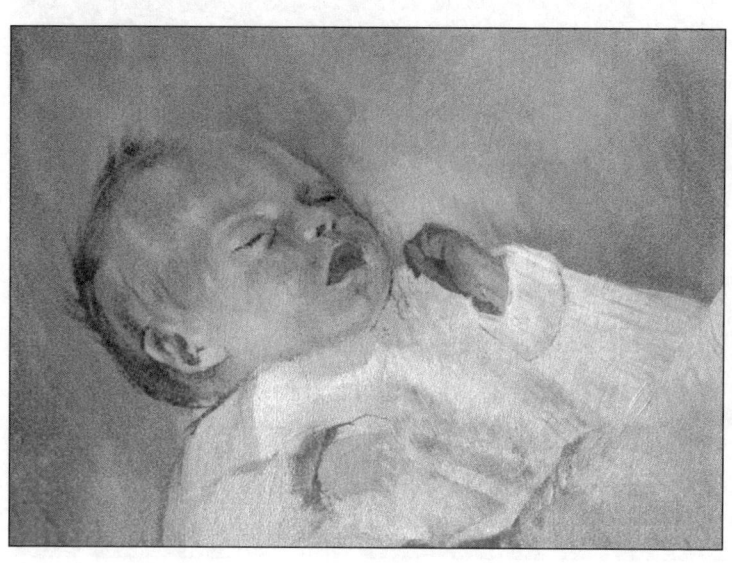

96 a & b: *Dorelia*

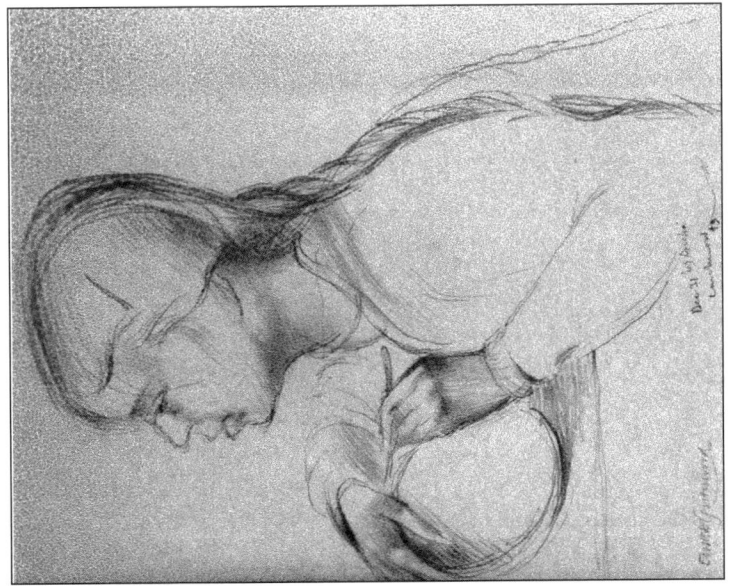

96 c & d: Dorelia

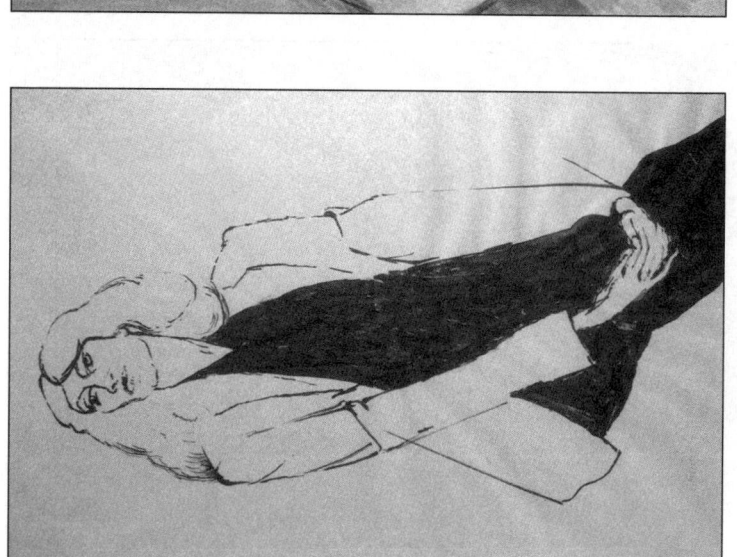

98a: Dorelia

103: *'A British Soldier'*
Pencil. 1945. Private Collection.

104: 'The Garden Party'

105: 'A Suffolk Mill'

106 & 107: The French Villages

108: 'The Hermitage Courtyard'

109: 'Evening Bonfire'

110: College days etchings, 1933

✺ V ✺
ADDITIONAL WORKS

The following selection of drawings, made from several thousands, have been chosen to illustrate a serious study of nature – drawings made for their own sake.

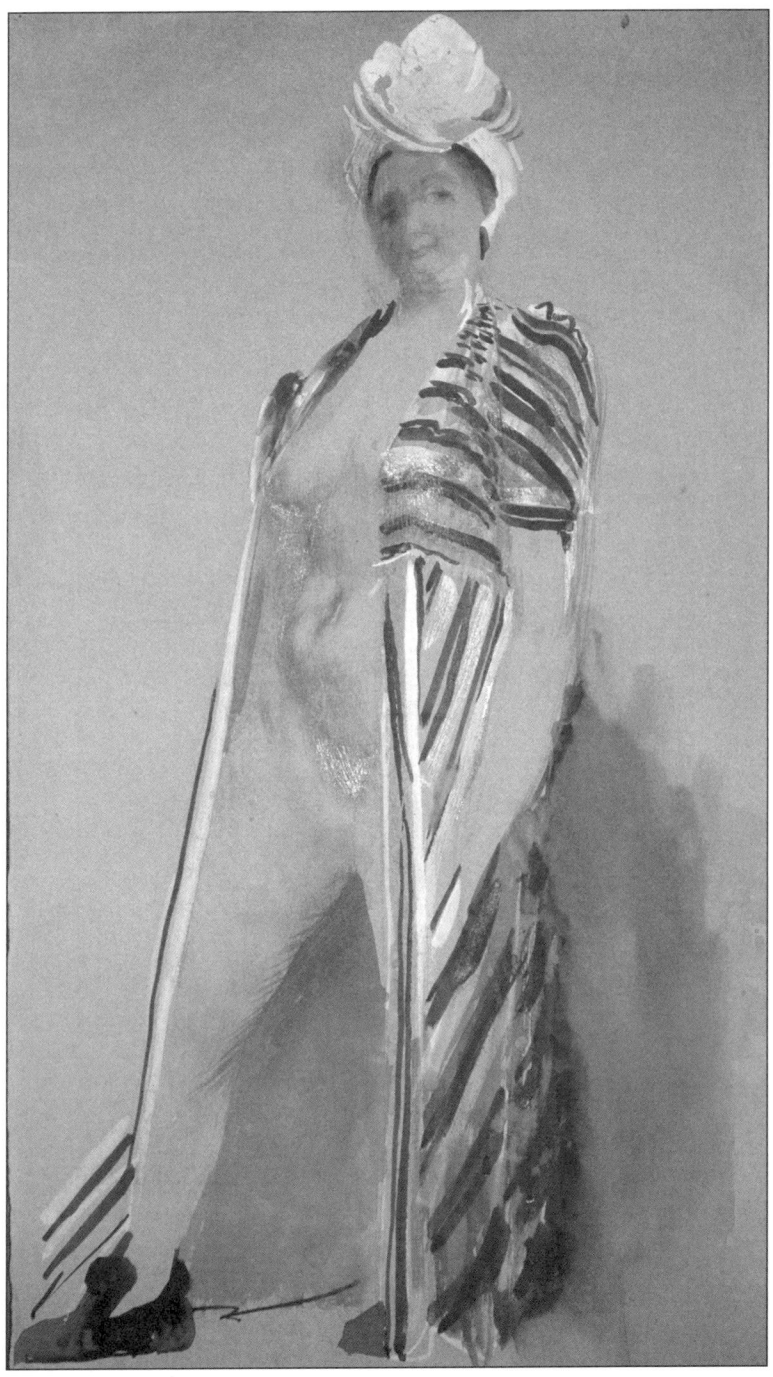

My Mother

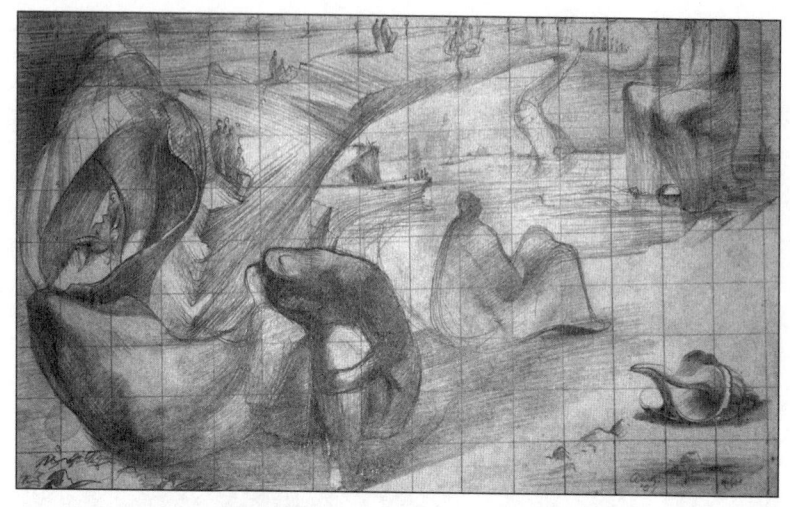

A second study for 'The Planets'

'Spring Flowers'

French Landscape

Chateaux Biron

Portrait of Digby

Church Tower, Cyprus

Houses in Cyprus

CONCLUSION

There is never a conclusion to anything; but looking back nearly ninety years leads inevitably to making an assessment of the experiences and influences which have been of paramount importance in shaping my life and character.

It was early in my art school days that I began to think about the meaning and purpose of life and, in a vague way, what I wanted to do with mine. I felt the inadequacy of the intellectual philosophy of the official churches, least of all the belief in miracles or superstition or the practices and complicated ritual of the Roman church. The leadership that would even begin to provide me with what I was subconsciously looking for, in spite of the years in which the Greenwood phalanx attended services at a Methodist church up to the time I began studying, was not there. As I have indicated elsewhere, serious study of art was not confined to the acquisition of a particular craft or skill but included the reading over a much wider field, which I continue to enjoy, especially now that the continuation of the creation of paintings is no longer possible other than in a very restricted way.

I now know that my first reading of the book on the Renaissance set the seal on my future interests and predilections which was to design, and select, from the natural world of plants and animals forms with which to produce a picture. I remember so well how my first attempts at figure composition, which consisted of nudes in a landscape, invoked ribald comments from the student body. There has always been, since the earliest years, the wish to paint a picture that would say more than a competent reproduction of fact, which early training set out to do.

My most ambitious composition which attempted to do this was made at college. This was a long narrow panel (a format I have since used many times) containing people on a riverside, which included a back view of my sister Lilian, wearing my hat! Which reminds me, during my last conversation with my sister, Lilian, she often said what a wonderful comfort and understanding companion her daughter had always been. The panel also included a pair of fighting swans. I enclosed in a letter to Sir William Rothenstien my only copy of this work when writing to him about possible employment; the result was negative, and I lost my photograph!

Serious study of painting and literature developed as I matured. I am particularly thankful for this second interest now. It was a natural thing to turn to Greek literature after drawing architecture; the last of these being a compulsory subject on the art school curriculum, so I read Greek plays. I read Plato, feeling my way tentatively into a glimpse of the classical world, as I continue to do. In the 1960s I had my interest in philosophy rekindled in a strange way.

It was in the 1960s that my colleague, inspector of French, and I were on our way to Strasbourg University to tutor two small groups of secondary school teachers of French and Art. At the Gare Saint-Lazare we hired a cab to take us across Paris and, sitting on the back seat, I had a perfect view of the neck of the taxi driver. During the drive across the city I had time to make a few sketches including our driver. As he chatted on, he finally came out with 'I was once a painter', and a statement by Schopenhauer along the lines of, 'Art was given to us to console us to reality'. This led me back to Schopenhauer. Although, in recent reading, I have been unable to find the exact quotation, I have found many relevant ones that express similar thoughts. An aspect of aesthetics includes the imagination which is expressed as the work of impregnating the empirical with concepts, but leaving the imagination free to experience the inexpressible in aesthetics, so the word 'aesthetics' becomes more and more difficult to understand.

The Parisian taxi driver's casual comment reminded me of the London taxi driver who became 'Mastermind'. I wonder what the circumstances were that two men with considerable potential for much more than just driving a taxi had found themselves doing just that. They were probably great readers with retentive memories. But the Parisian driver gave me plenty to think about, and more reading has given me a firmer basis on which to judge works of art. This in turn has stimulated my pleasure in reading, heightening the quality of my awareness in contemplating the work of the masters.

Aesthetics has been a philosophical issue from Plato to the present time. It has been (still is) a difficult word to define. In my first reading I thought the definition 'The philosophy of the beautiful' was complete and all embracing, but now I know otherwise.

The word 'beautiful' reminds me of a particularly sensitive passage from 'The one thing needful' (*GS* 276) in *Nietzsche's*

Voice in which Nietzsche writes '. . . I want to learn more and more to see as beautiful what is necessary in things, then I shall be one of those who make things beautiful . . .'

* * *

We measure time as the interval between known events, so events measure time for us. We also assess time from physical factors; through archaeology we know that the sun warming us today also shone on the dinosaurs. But this long period is a mere fragment in the lifetime of the world. If mankind is measured on this timescale he was not, in the beginning, much more than a grain of dust. But this grain of dust, in some incomprehensible way, acquired a brain, so this speck of humanity, from being a grain of dust travelling in space and time, has become the possible destructor of its own world.

The rapid advance of technology has made the earth less secure and permanent than we once thought it was. The world is in a restless turmoil of international strife. The possession of nuclear power is now being used by many countries with the revenue to spend on such an unproductive and expensive product, which expenditure could help feed 800 million hungry people. Earthquakes on land and under the sea, together with hurricanes, are causing great distress to a rapidly growing world population.

In my search for the exact quotation of Schopenhauer to which I was taken back by my Parisian taxi driver's casual remark, I did find many relevant passages which made me think about the three important words, namely art, console and reality.

Philosophers find the question of the arts a necessary, vital subject for thought and in dissertation. One of the greatest was Plato, who characteristically tries to find the root cause for the existence of an unchanged creative energy such as the arts. Imperfect individual things come and go but this does not affect the fundamental order in the universe. Concepts are mental constructions that we make in order to grasp reality in general terms. The artist is able to detach himself from the world during the time of creative activity; it is then that perceptions and imagination help to convert the conventional into a significant, sometimes great image. So, the great painting is the result of three factors: the object, the artist and the influence of intuition. The latter can be understood as the immediate perception of the mind without reasoning. So it would seem, in trying to understand reality, we pass from the material to a metaphysical state during which true order, arrangement, selection, retention, amplification and colour coalesce to form what we call a painting. 'The genius alone can bestow dignity on human life because through him, the one will achieves its goal of self-glorification in works of Art'. (Nietzsche)

This attempt to produce a summary of my memoirs is proving more difficult than I thought it would be. It leads one into corners of memory once thought long forgotten. Our move from Broad Street was the conclusion of an idyllic life. It had, with the environment, the downland, the feeling of living time in all its aspects. As the work aesthetic becomes more obtuse, complicated and indefinable, the experience obtained from a deep appreciation of the world, of all its animals and flowers culminates in the ultimate reality, freed from time and space.

It was never my intention to enlarge on the original thoughts regarding my motives and ambitions in art. The analysis of reasons for the attempt to find a basic, convincing philosophy appertaining to creativity was made for my better understanding of the work to which I have devoted my life.

Philosophy is the concern of philosophers. They do a lot of thinking, writing and lecturing in universities, with the aim of solving the many speculations and theories concerning the world and the life on it. There is no agreement among many great thinkers, since Aristotle, about fundamental issues that have occupied their time and intellectual powers, but many truths filter through time with scraps of wisdom which unconsciously improve the understanding of the many.

Music and poetry have contributed a great deal to my enjoyment. For a short time I tried to play the piano but soon discovered I had no aptitude. But words, because of my reading – especially of plays and poetry, offered more as an addition to paintings; each assisting the other. When we moved into Brushings this important event produced a period of emotional tranquillity as we began to make it our own. It was on the early mornings while I was out with our dog, when the downs were free of people, when these downland slopes owned themselves and their secrets, that I felt the need and the wish to write down, in an organised, concentrated form, responses to the imaginative concepts that these walks provoked. Memoirs unveil the progression of the individual's path along the road of life, so I make no apology for concluding this part of my memoirs with a few verses which were made to satisfy this wish.

CONCLUSION

On moving into Brushings

I heard the lightest footfall on the sodden grass
From shadows passed the sound of hurrying feet
From which the thought of an eternal spring can never pass
Or winter cold forever linger in the ancient street
To smother the sighing silences of my heart,
Or still my breath from lifting the curtain of your
Soul, to shift the silver mist of vistas quite apart.
Along the muddy track the blossoming hills were green.
A German helmet[1] on a vine clad fence was seen
The ruins of a convent house, crumbling in the light
Reflected back the sun in whose eternal warmth
We live and move, you and I, creatures of this hour
Must mingle, share each breath, or else we never flower.

---

[1] The reference to a German helmet is connected with the booby trap my late friend James Martin fell into causing the explosion which severely damaged his right leg causing a perpetual limp. These lines were written with war experiences very much in mind.

The Downland Hawk

My hawk, harbinger of the morn, Horus, God of
The sun is but an oscillating movement on
The cooling, chilly breeze, it drops to earth only
To soar again, a fragment in its claws.
Morning is my crucible of thought into which the
rising sun's consuming fire of crimson heat goes
creeping through a vale of a blue grey sea where mystic
islands of the copse clad hills are born.
My hawk passes as night sweeps into day
spreading a golden dawn over the leafless way.

The Grandfather Clock

The Grandfather clock has chimed away the restless hours
of sleep, and my wakeful dog in the misty cold of dawn
is sadly barking, while on his swaying
perch the pheasant croaks towards the reluctant day.
As the night lights of early morn, in which my thoughts
Like lines of poesy, as through an hour glass drain away
    the hours.
As softly, the reign of day supplants the sheet of night
And the faintly mirrored ecstasy of joy reflects the
Measure of my growing misery – but listen
the thrushes are beginning to sign –
My darling, your thrushes are beginning to sing.

CONCLUSION

Brushings in Spring

Cold sits in November
Darkness fits December
A change in January
When the cold earth cracks open wide for a
    warming soil, its richness to provide,
ecstatic, with soothing showers, and a symphony
    of song for spring – a celebration
while the barn owl sleeps
As the green corn grows
When warm, blue mists herald a coming day,
    with birds and flowers to delight,
adorning a newly awakened earth with Flora's
    gifts, made to mitigate the worldwide,
    manmade, miseries of men.

Blackthorn in February

The hedgerow blackthorn in funeral dress, like a smudge
    of charcoal along the boundary ran. Responding to a
    springtime call, a shower of flowers, as a coat of white
    over the
blackthorn throws.
A sign for earth to rise from slumber, sloth, and sleep to
    life again.

On Finding Brushings

Upon a hill top the trees stood tall and grey
Beneath the hill
An ancient dwelling, wrapped in a shroud of
  mossy green like an aged monument lay.
The garden overgrown with weeds.
The house, covered with a creeper to the eaves
  lay slowly breathing with a sighing
sound like a spiders web, with a fly entwined.
Broken gates, no longer from the narrow lane
  the land confined.
A lonely, mystic house.
Upon the air a distant dirge did sound.
A cavern small, dismal and dark had a cold,
  inhospitable gloom.
But a sense, intuitive and strong
Whispered of better days long gone.
Yet, lingering in a musty air, a promise
  of – resurrection.

Mountain Cottage

Two tiny bedrooms, candle lit topped the rickety stairs,
Thro' a chilly night our palliasses of straw were warm.
On knees, finger nails scraping ice from windows
Transformed the twilight eve of green, into a morn of white.
As the Queen, with retinue of stars drifted away,
The day before us was virgin born.

This scintillating sheen, unsullied and stark
Was studied in startled silence when the empty world
Suddenly sprung into life as a sleek red-brown phantom-
Like body, thro' open gate, into the woods and was gone.
Years later, we relished reflections on Reynard's realm
Reflections on Fox hunting too!

She sits, a solitary unloved soul in sad squalor.
One flickering, spitting candle inadequate for darning
Socks outworn
On the kitchen range, hand-scrubbed, the day's washing
Drip dried
As dismal darkness dissolves into vacant nothingness
Of mind
An unpaid drudge works on, pale face, much lined,
A wife, a mother, a slave and no one cries as in a
Wayside Chapel graveyard now she lies.

My Moon

The evening sun clothing the clouds with a
golden, shimmering light.
That surrendered to her majesty who rules the mystic night
Who rises, slowly, solemnly with unhurried stealth
Across a violet realm of undisputed wealth
The spring awaiting trees
Scantily clothed in leaves
Like lace against the evening sky,
The soothing exudation of a summer night
While I, in trance-like gaze did lie
A youth in dreaming,
Did marvel at the power of poetry to
Change vulgarian life into one in fairyland.

Long have the sciences held the arts in thrall
Travelling in space is now, no trouble at all.
With wealth from the greedy taxman's haul,
We travel in space, when much of the race
Dies for the want of a loaf.
When once the hallowed, mystic space was broken
Heaven became the place for man's scientific litter
But the son of Philomel has hushed the noise of day
So my serenade to the Queen of heaven was heard
By the scattered stars a million miles away.

CONCLUSION

Wine

When time was still young and Bacchus a growing boy
Olympians decreed, that Bacchus must be God
Of wine, to soften tragedy and grief with joy.
Only the boy remembered the Elysian Fields of Paradice,
  the banks of flowers reflected in pools of night,
The sunlit groves of scented trees
Were the holy realms of the Gods' immortal might
The way of life changed with industries gain
The influence of Bacchus gradually grew, as the
Product of his homeland, spread to nations new.
When into a man Bacchus grew, the rites of love
Flowered and prospered too.
The Bacchanalia with riotously festive dance
Did welcome Baccante to love and delight.

The vine, heaven sent bliss, was born to assuage
And ease the pain and toil of man
Whose labour, this warm autumn day has seen the
Harvest press, awaiting to possess, the tumbril's
Gift to measure, and crush the grapes by night and day
To start another vintage year for the farmer's pleasure, who
  watches the labourers with heavy
Baskets on stalwart shoulders tipping torrents of purple
  treasure into the waiting vats.
The farmer's hands are large and browned from
Work, to win a living from the stony ground
But, O! the joy in spring to see the rows and rows of vines
All neatly trimmed and turning green
The vine, heaven sent plant was seen, in the beautiful
Harvest of the new harvest wine.

– 30 August 2006

Remembered

The celebration was full of youthful joy
And all the world our festival partook
As stars of eve glowed in a dark blue sky
Her speaking eyes with happiness did look
With palpitations of an unknown kind.
We sat with anxious, doubtful thoughts in mind.

I remembered well her bright red ballroom gown
No candelabra in Blenheim or Versailles ever gave
Such a warming light to our small room.
Down the hill lay a colourless provincial town
Waiting a not too distant time, when its minimal soul
Would be sacrificed on the altar of modernity.

From time our loving hours were stolen.
Those hours were sweet, magic moments
When all our idyllic days and years were golden
Long after the lovely red rose had become a
Snow White bloom in eternity.

CONCLUSION

Oscar

Since time began, the evil deeds of man
Had never touched the Emperor's dog
Where in the Palace Garden lies his tomb
Recording his devotion night and day
To dogs of every size and hue
Know when the master's love is due.

In every soul, virtues may not linger
In every canine heart, slumber sleeps alert
Anxiously awaiting his master's call
For help or company
In darkest cloud, or misty night
An intruder's stealth is put to flight.

History and Literature, both in
Fact and fiction, speak fondly of
Individual services given –
The trained house dog
Or vicious in the hunt
The sporting hound
The expert with his sheep
Or, on the hearthrug fast asleep
Dreaming, of peaceful pleasure when
We all live and love together.

A pause in an author's writing day,
Can with humour
Observe his canine's entertaining play
With a favourite toy.
But one of the most enchanting things with
Oscar, is the sudden burst of frenzied joy
And pleasure – when we love and live together.

– 20 August 2006

Loneliness

Much of our conscious thinking is
Done alone.
Oppressive, resentful thoughts, picturing our sleeping in
Slumbers deep
We sleep alone.
With anxieties, with apprehension with the approach
Of a coming day
We wake alone.
To find evil tumours have never passed away
In sleep.
In loneliness, Majestic Memnon, mourning, gazes across
Sands infinity, in haunting dreams of memory.
I dream alone
As physique experiencing pain crumples,
So distant, seems each youthful day
When seldom did steps stumble to hinder progress
Or allay
The harboured secrets of the mind make each
An island to mankind.
A loneliness
When first I become a conscious thing
I'm alone.
Now an old bird with broken wing
All our injured lives can bring
Is loneliness.

During my Presidency of the Royal Watercolour Society we had the honour and privilege of welcoming Her Majesty

CONCLUSION

Queen Elizabeth II on November 11th 1980 to open the new Bankside Gallery. Shortly before this event my friend, Harry Ecclestone, sent me a calendar and as it included the date on which Her Majesty officially opened Bankside, and because of the motto printed on the bottom, I kept it. It must have been during the clearing of Brushings that this particular leaf was lost. So imagine my pleasure when, on receiving an appreciative note from my neighbour, Jan Worden, concerning the delivery of her copy of *The Last of Seven* (Part I), she included the scrap of paper I thought was lost.

I found this incident, after twenty-five years, quite a remarkably survival of the past and worthy of recording in these last pages by a reproduction of the lost leaf.

This was on the calendar at work the day the Queen opened the Gallery!

Thoughts on freedom

These thoughts on concepts of reality, which began with a Parisian taxi driver's quotation from Schopenhauer were, in my mind, linked to our use of freedom. When freedom degenerates into licence, and diminishes self respect with self control and dignity, the worst tendencies grow and proliferate in people. When every domestic need is easily acquired, which in a highly technical age is a long list of needs or wants, when all these things are so easily acquired and nothing much to save for except perhaps longer holidays abroad, there is good reason to think that these affluent social conditions would stimulate a greater responsibility from people, to respect others with good manners and courtesy, but unfortunately the reverse is true.

The moral standards of a nation are reflected in its government.

POSTSCRIPT

(June–October 2006)

The Waiting Room

The journey in the ambulance was quite pleasant. Glimpses I had of the spring countryside were quite a revelation to one who could only venture out occasionally. The blackthorn hedges were heavy with white blossom, sheep were lazily grazing forming a familiar part of the spring green meadowland.

The local council was trying with determination to mask recent domestic housing which had the varied, and all too common indifference in its architecture. Some of the building was crowded and wisely screened from the road by generous tree planting. This included some forest examples, chestnut, beech, birch to smaller trees and shrubs, the hawthorns whose red and white was a delight amongst them.

But the urban environment, in general, wore a rather tired, uninspired complexion indicating a hurried piecemeal development. This was emphasised by the nineteenth-century manse built entirely of flint, with Flemish gables and the nearby contemporary parish church, until quite recently situated in a country area, but now, suffocated by hundreds of closely packed houses in what appeared to be served by a labyrinth of roads.

Where did the inhabitants of these dwellings work? Very few, as in the past, walked to their place of employment. Now you drive the car out of the garage, carport or, if neither, from a cemented area covering the front garden. The visual effect of the latter produces a chaotic mess to the street. This confusion is made worse when the back garden terminates at the road boundary where the original fencing has worn out or broken down and been replaced by the residents who must express their individuality by erecting a fence quite different from their neighbours next-door. The result is even more disturbing when broken wooden fencing, brick sections high and low, paling, etc; the occupants totally unaware of the need for uniformity only achieved by the repetition of one unit.

Two other examples of this all too common practice, this form of unconscious vandalism (encouraged by DIY) were noticed in a row of Edwardian cottages where every original front door in the street had been replaced by one of a different design and colour. In the same locality a charming row of Victorian dwellings which once had a repetition of one form of fenestration – diamond panes – had all been changed, one by one, to something entirely different from the next dwelling. The original glazing only remained in the attics, the dormer windows suggesting these little rooms were never used, but those dormers indicated the charm and unity which was obviously the architect's intention – little thoughts destroying the large one! And thus my journey continued, interspersed by casual remarks from the nurse to driver, into an unlovely suburbia until, with a rattling of clips and chains from all safety devices on the wheelchairs, we were lowered to road level: a manoeuvre most competently executed.

POSTSCRIPT

So, in a wheeled chair, I was pushed to the dental consultant's department, a new experience of considerable proportions. The waiting area was fully occupied so I was abandoned in the doorway in full view of fifteen or more people. One patient had a modern hairdo, glued into a number of jet black spikes like a hedgehog. Another patient too, equally tall if not even taller, characterised by his baseball cap worn straight but looking too small on such a big man but on returning to the reception desk, after a very short consultation, the cap had been twisted round, the large peak now covering his thick neck making him look absurd. A third man, sitting close to me, was a fidget intermittently crossing his legs to display, apparently for my special benefit, his large new trainers on huge feet, the soles tilted vertically showing how new they were by being spotless, so new; did they pinch a bit? Probably, the laces were undone. Entertainment for all was provided by a young child owned by an almost equally young mother. The pair were sitting next to the man wearing the new trainers so he reaped full benefit from the antics of the child who started off by bouncing up and down on mother's lap accompanied by shouts of excited laughter. But soon it tired, was put down and began searching in the shopping bag for something to eat, of a sweet nature. Then, when prevented from this activity, began bawling lustily expressing its annoyance and petulance until a mature matron brought peace and quiet by a subtle manipulation of her person into a welcoming pose, and a toy!

The next character to occupy the stage was another tall person, a woman in her thirties I should think. Her high-heeled, pointed shoes announced her interest which was obviously 'fashion'. Her diaphanous silky dress was high at the sides and drooped low at front and back producing a most original hemline. Cards and forms of different sizes and colours passed between her and the receptionist before she made a dignified exit. As her ladyship floated out between two rows of waiting people, all with such varied expressions on inquisitive faces, the great eternal thought about the meaning and purpose of life confronted me. I wondered what were these people thinking about other than the condition of their teeth? The continued increase in world population is making it more difficult for many to keep alive, never mind happy. Starving, under-fed people with no future prospects are all too many for a new millennium. The basic, fundamental, instinct for all living creatures is to copulate to keep alive their own species, with tragic results for the world. The human race is the only species to grow in uncontrolled numbers to the detriment of all other creatures who, because of shortage of food and reduced space, are on the decline. So, unawares my audience caused me to think about problems which will concern future generations more and more as the century advances. Most of the people in the waiting area were young enough to be conscious of the growing world condition but technology is placing attractive alternatives to thinking in the hands of many.

The media thrives on the revenue from popular entertaining and absorbing programmes broadcast. Those with an inexhaustible appeal are dramas and romances, especially those with a sexual/love bias. Television can, and does make the most of this human predilection for easily digested fare.

So people survive on pictures to an extent as never before. Images and aspects of life personal, private, intimate including factors which adults once thought it better children should not know.

They are automatically informed now, especially those whose over indulgent parents provide children with their own television sets, mobile phones and other equipment and all this expenditure after the car is bought, taxed, insured and the mortgage paid added to holidays abroad. The time of 'child innocence' a popular subject in Victorian paintings has gone – if it ever existed.

A sudden call from the dentist's assistant put an end to my meandering thoughts.

The Barn

Looking out from little earth into infinity produces an experience of wonder, mystic mental meanderings into that timeless, dimensionless space ever-changing colour we call the sky.

The sky is never alone, always entertaining an infinite number of guests from morning to night, always on the move coming and going restlessly to an unknown destination. The metamorphosis is equally mysterious making of solidity a form of short duration before melting away.

The occupants of this infinitude are continuously, with patience and repetitive information, enlightening souls on earth with instruction and knowledge for those who can listen and understand.

The mariner's dependence on the stars, moon and weather conditions were his main assistance when travelling on the sea until science and technology invented an almost infallible method of moving from one continent to another in comparative safety.

Apart from the practical aspect of considering the firmament the sun, moon and stars have always inspired an entirely different type of sensibility to think and work in regions of mental activity.

Poetry (prose is another thing altogether using words factually with a limited descriptive meaning) creates visions which are felt, dimly cognised with ideas which appear unrelated but contribute to the whole, an aesthetic pleasure few enjoy.

Evening on earth is transformed by light from sun and moon, under fixed or fluctuating rays caused by the clouds who, performing their infinite changes are a weather vane telling us winter has gone, spring is on the way with soft warm rain for the thirsty earth and crops until harvest day.

The barn, dominating the farmyard group of characteristic architecture of a Romanesque abbey complex, stands in a dignified calm grey, anticipating the coming time of dominating day, when the autumn carts come rumbling in, with corn and hay.

– 6 October 2006

The Dream

A compensating advantage of going to bed early is that it provides a comfortable place in which to read, to think, to reminisce. When a satisfactory arrangement of supporting pillows has been made and you are warm, with an adequate reading light, then there is nothing better with which to close the day, than with a book.

Every book written constitutes an idea, or ideas, often for enlightenment concerned with aspects of history (either ancient or more recent) the arts and sciences; or for entertainment such as humour. But history helps relate most subjects to one another. One of these giving me great lasting pleasure is poetry.

'We are but stuff as dreams are made on our little life is rounded in a sleep'. A rather philosophical thought lies at the root of 'Every man is an island'. The dream remains a mystery. In spite of investigators, philosophers, and others, no one has yet provided a convincing explanation for the dream. Freud's insistence on sex being a fundamental factor in human behaviour has yet to be substantiated.

Why are dreams so varied, so persistent, so long-lasting? Why is it that they can remain in the memory for years. A dream I had at the age of about ten is one that has become more and more vivid as the years pass and which I tried to visualise in Part I of my memoirs. Another featuring an enormous triumphal arch constructed entirely of cheap breeze blocks, in a pale blue charcoal colour, plain and undecorated. I have lived with this image for years.

Imagination such as Magritte's was able to organise this imagery into pictures of an unreal world giving rise to an aspect of painting shared by several artists such as Salvador Dali. Towards the end of the nineteenth century a number of movements were being made by artists and designers to replace Classicism, the influence of which had lasted too long. Art Nouveau was one of these fashions, Gaudi's cathedral in Barcelona being the largest single work in this mode.

One of my most recent dreams took place last night, August 24th. In it, it seemed as if a curtain was raised on a familiar interior, one reminiscent of a room connected with my youth but mixed with Brushings Farm House. It had a large inglenook with a small fire burning in a tiny, conventional grate.

The room was littered with a miscellany of papers and books which seemed to be related in a vague way to me.

Eileen went over to the fire, which had no flames but only red cinders were in the grate, to throw on a piece of screwed-up paper which bounced back falling on the carpet, too far away for her to notice. I picked up the paper, went over to the fire, cautiously, but there was no heat to avoid.

Then looking up to a window I saw that a car had driven to the door quite close. Eileen said, 'What colour is it?' looking through the Crittall-type window (which I hate). I said 'A warm grey', her reply was 'It must be Miss Laidler.' This caused some alarm to us both. I remember the white table cloth with a much worn lace fringe with a hole in one side (something I had remarked on just before leaving Lakeside). Miss Laidler (the late Principal of Battersea College of Domestic Science who became a great friend) appeared in my dream as a disembodied presence but with a ghostlike reality.

On coming into the room she said that the windscreen wiper on her car was broken, and she showed me a nondiscernible, almost invisible, object in a hand that wasn't there.

Saying she was cold she went to the inglenook carrying over a minimal stool much too small for her, in order to sit by a nonexistent fire, opposite the small modern fireplace in which we had tried to burn paper.

It would seem that Miss Laidler had been invited to lunch with us but no preparations of any kind had been made, just paper and books covered the table. Opposite the Crittall window stood a chest of drawers, similar to that at Lakeside, but taller – it being used as a sideboard almost covered with detritus.

I found myself walking towards it when a cold hand brought me back into the world, a world without a future, another kind of living which will only have the mark of uniform mediocrity. In fact the hand was not so cold, it was the hand of a carer with a lovely warm nature by whom I did not expect to be awakened.

Whether regularly, intermittently, vaguely or vividly, whether short or long lasting, I think we must all have dreams in some form or another during a lifetime.

In early Jewish biblical history, the dream is written about as being interpreted by a soothsayer, magicians and prophets all with superstition to misinterpret and mislead, an excellent example being the story of Belshazzar's Feast. The dream is like a second life, reflecting in sleep events, experiences and unfulfilled desires which are hidden or overlaid by the conscious daily pursuits of living.

Dreams can, and often are the source of works of art, or provide the content for painting which transcends pen or the optical organisation of subject matter. Dreams stimulate imagination, especially in poetic form; the musical rhythm carries a number of creative ideas vaguely logically connected, but essential for the unity of the whole. Coleridge's 'Kubla Khan' is a wonderful example of this in which visions to marvel at for themselves occupy the mind in realms of delightful fantasy.

A relatively small number of paintings contain – if you are sensitive to apprehend, or feel the presence of it – a concentration of underlying motif which is of the painting but in no way *is* the painting. Because of the two parts one is seen in terms of colour, tone and design while the content cannot be so seen; the aesthetic is in no way related to intelligence but is a way the spiritual faculty is only stimulated and brought into conscious existence by the contemplation of special works of art where it exists. Some of Turner's late works have this lasting quality which makes them great creations and separates them from illustrations no matter how competent they be.

The final dream is the last dream, the most secret part of our ego, the images of which remain locked in the dreamer's mind, shared only with eternity. I suppose the dream is a review of a lifetime and emphasises the emotional, disasters and delights which in their power of producing a type of revision, a simulation of reality, an imprint on the mind. These night pictures offer a short-lived knowledge, forming another dimension in space, the subconscious images produced by a second life through dreams in space; they are only perceived fragmentally, infrequently, seldom understood except by the intuition of some poets who create a mystical, rhythmic language which expresses but a fragment of the necessary understanding of dreams or life.

A frightening remembrance of things past is not so much experienced in the dream as in the nightmare. 'She' is represented as an evil monster, suffocating the peaceful sleeper producing a horrible haunting fear, the incubus, the persistent terror of the sleeping. This is a phenomenon which has been powerfully used by artists. Goya created some pictures difficult to understand if you fail to relate them to the horrors of the Inquisition during the lifetime of Goya.

These, with other pictures organise and externalise the man-made misery imposed by a Christian cult. Such inhumanity has many outlets political as well as religious in which the worst characteristics of men become manifest. Many of the works of Munch express a similar pessimism, an outlook on society which has coloured his work, from boyhood and through life. James Stephens' Preface to Ruth Pitter's *A Trophy of Arms* (1936) is a most penetrating exposition of what constitutes a lasting work of art, as distinct from the many, which are not.

What is the mind as distinct from the brain? The brain has dimensions and weight, it has a location. The faculties, thinking, willing and perceiving, are distinguished from the body, the intellectual faculty distinct from the will, emotion, memory.

The mind perceives an infinite number of concepts, many of which are trivial, unimportant but little ones frequently lead to big conclusions. The mind is invisible, does not have any corporeal attributes, therefore it is not difficult to think of the mind as a separate entity from the brain.

The mind is unknowable, invisible, its presence only made real in its capacity to create or govern actions, thinking, feeling and emotions each of which have an infinite number of permutations. Intuition makes possible results which are not the product of forethought, reasoning or intelligence. You perceive by intuition – immediate insight into unpredictable ends.

The soul is less comprehensible than the mind and is a most ephemeral concept since we do not attribute any of the functions of the mind to the soul. So how do we use the word soul? chiefly by religious organisations in vague disputes/discussions associated with the idea of immortality in which the immortality of the soul is a key issue.

How long historically has this idea occupied the minds of men? Are human beings the only creatures on this earth with a 'soul to save'? Is this derived from the Christian belief in a heaven and hell, both of which, in one way or another, are to be found in most religions in the world? Mysticism, superstition and fear have governed the lives of men for many centuries contributing very little fundamental happiness to the believers.

– September 2006

The Dining Room

The view from a door, in the bay window, which was the width of the dining room was pleasant. A wide expanse of well-maintained lawn separated the two wings of these late eighteenth century red brick buildings. The good quality of the brickwork helped to date the structures and showed up the poor standard of contemporary craftsmanship in recent repair and alteration work.

The generous quadrangle contained well-pruned shrubs and flowering trees symmetrically planted. Just off-centre a fountain surrounded by closely clipped conifers faintly echoed the great English gardens, which is where the comparison stopped. It did not, could not, express more about itself than what it was, a pleasant screen between two parallel buildings. It breathed no message, as does the White Garden at Sissinghurst, but does help to sweeten the lives of the residents. As I watched the dandelion parachutes carrying their single seed drift by in the sunlight I thought of the millions of human beings who drift by with similar aimless goals, pass from sunshine into darkness, leaving no evidence to posterity that they had ever existed, except, for a short time after, in the minds of others.

But the garden and surrounding buildings on three sides of a square do attract birds. Throughout history birds have played a prominent part in an imaginative and symbolic language. The dove, raven, phoenix, eagle, swan and pigeon were, and still are, in a minor way, used for the communication of ideas and messages. Even so they were not, or were very seldom, thought of as special creatures to be given any particular care with the exception of the purpose-built, medieval pigeon and egg-production houses, designed to accommodate hundreds of birds who became a real pest when, on release, they settled on a nearby farmer's crops.

St Francis was the first European known to have called attention to the need to protect and love birds. As with so many aspects of human behaviour, among the number of people who care about birds there are those who find pleasure in shooting them as a sport. One of the better things that the past decade has seen is the Royal Society for the Protection of Birds. Our interest has grown since our small patio became the means of observing the birds which come to feed. Their number and variety have increased since regular feeding began, providing great pleasure from the study of their habits and behaviour. The following visitors have come to our various food supplies: pigeons, wagtails, magpies, chaffinch, starlings, sparrows, thrush, blackbird and collared dove.

POSTSCRIPT

Then I turned my back on the garden and looked into and around the dining room, which was empty of course, and thought of those who at appropriate times come to eat and drink. They were all burdened with a handicap of some sort, yet all were ready to laugh – a pent-up emotional condition we all experience at some time. The number of men were outnumbered by the women.

The clientele would provide a Cruikshank, Rowlandson or best of all a Leonardo with perfect subjects on which they could record their immortality. The multiplicity of experiences which we all share, the level of fears, hopes and hates, the disappointments and conscious knowledge of failures and success are all etched, with many other things, indelibly stamped on all faces, which provide an insight into character.

But there are other things too. Sitting at my dining table which I call the 'Royal Box', as it commands a view of all but three of the total number of tables gives me an excellent view of the feet of the diners; and no pair of feet were rested in the same way. They were placed together, flat on the carpet, crossed under the chair, some on tiptoe, others on their heels, or one shoe off; some with their legs straight out with their feet hidden. I wonder what Freud would have made of this phenomenon?

When the tables are laid on immaculate linen and a small vase of artificial flowers added, they give a little colour to each table and the room in general. It provides a very attractive environment in which to enjoy food.

Bread, 'the staff of life', was only achieved after centuries of cultivation of the grass *triticum* produced a grain suitable for making bread. The corn was ground in a quern, the primitive origin of the wind and water mills which illustrate an aspect of the eighteenth and nineteenth century engineering skills in wood and metal. The remaining examples are now, wisely, being restored and in a few cases still being used for their original purpose, converting grain to flour to make bread.

For many years bread, and its almost countless permutations, was the food for thousands of people until development in communities and domestic activities increased the supply of food – keeping poultry, and farmers by breeding animals: the goat, sheep, cows and pigs.

Food production has been progressing for centuries, ever since the introduction of rhubarb by the Romans and the potato by Raleigh. But recent imports have included the tomato, grapefruit, kiwi fruit, spices and herbs.

Food can be thought of in a non-gustatory sense in the expression 'food for thought', but what is it that does the thinking? Is it the mind? The word 'thought' immediately transforms the emphasis from gustation to the metaphysical.

Flowers (plants) form the first of the three divisions into which Aristotle divides his investigations of life – animals and humans constituting the second and third parts. Flowers have always formed an important role in the development of humanity. Their role has been medicinal, culinary, decorative and ceremonial, as in weddings and funerals or, tokens of sympathy for a public tragedy.

Flowers – old ones – but especially new varieties are of great interest to the specialists working at Kew in the Botanical Gardens. Flowers have become an essential part of laying a table, whether for a banquet or a simple meal at home, so flowers appear on restaurant and dining room tables automatically. People have always found the need to collect or preserve things by embalming humans and animals; flowers are pressed and preserved in books for the information and pleasure they give. The use of flowers for commemorative purposes in France and other continental countries has given rise to an industry making metal flowers and bouquets for decorating graves. The results are often bizarre especially when the rusty and broken glass frames of photographs give the whole area a look of neglect.

Much poetry has been written about flowers from Chaucer onwards. They have always been and remain the gift of a lover as a token, a desire to move towards a special and life long relationship. The original nervous, emotional ecstasy is only once experienced, it only dissolves into a rich companionship once the many problems of life are shared. Flowers speak silently, a song without words.

—June 2006